THIS LOG BOOK BELONGS TO

DATE / LOCATION: _____

CONDITIONS

WEATHER:

WIND:

SHOOTING

FIREARM:

BULLET:

SEATING DEPTH:

POWDER:

GRAINS:

PRIMER:

BRASS:

DISTANCE:

OVERALL RESULTS

☆ ☆ ☆ ☆ ☆

NOTES

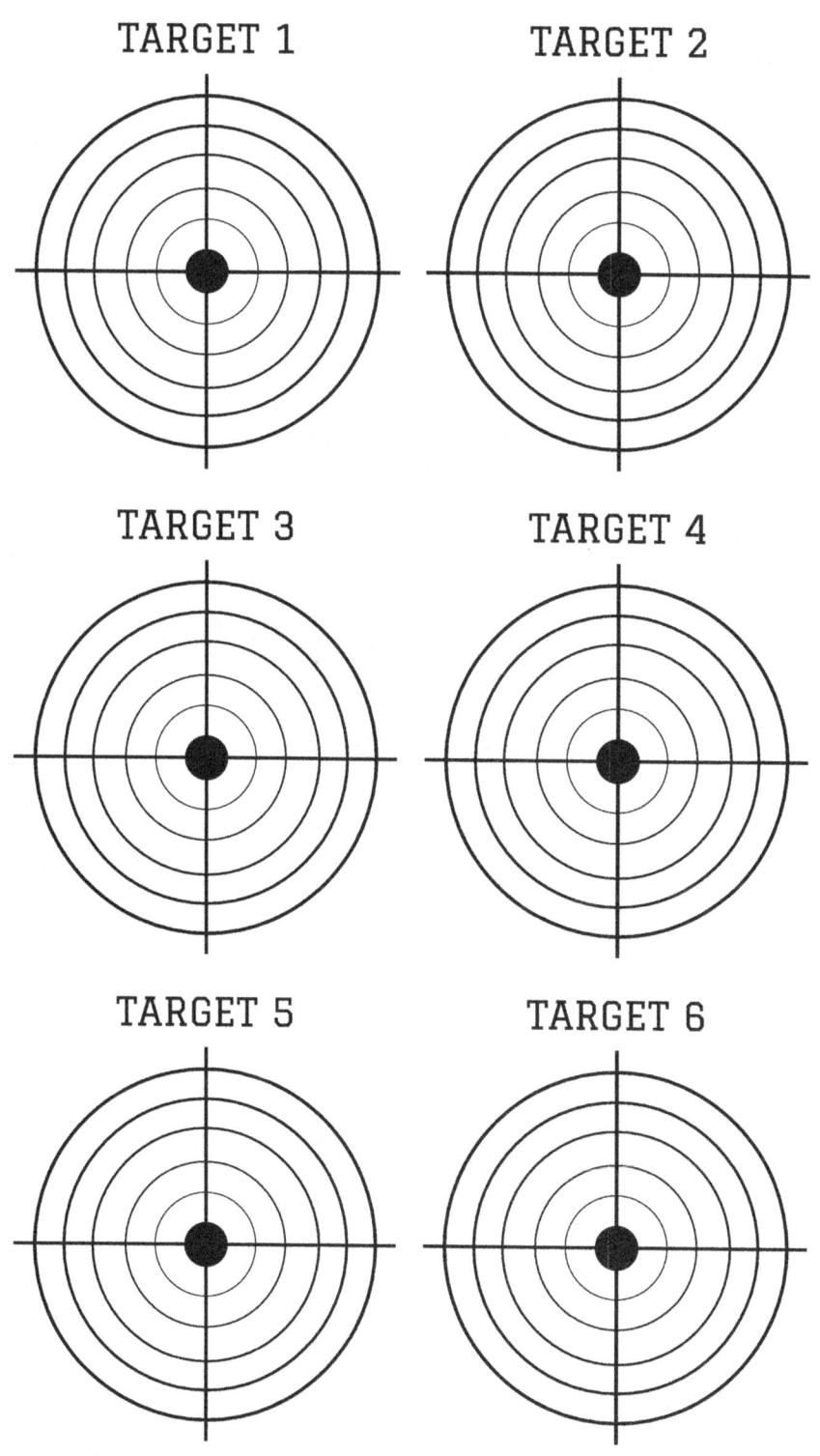

DATE / LOCATION: _____

CONDITIONS

WEATHER:

WIND:

SHOOTING

FIREARM:

BULLET: SEATING DEPTH:

POWDER: GRAINS:

PRIMER:

BRASS:

DISTANCE:

OVERALL RESULTS

★ ★ ★ ★ ★

NOTES

_____

_____

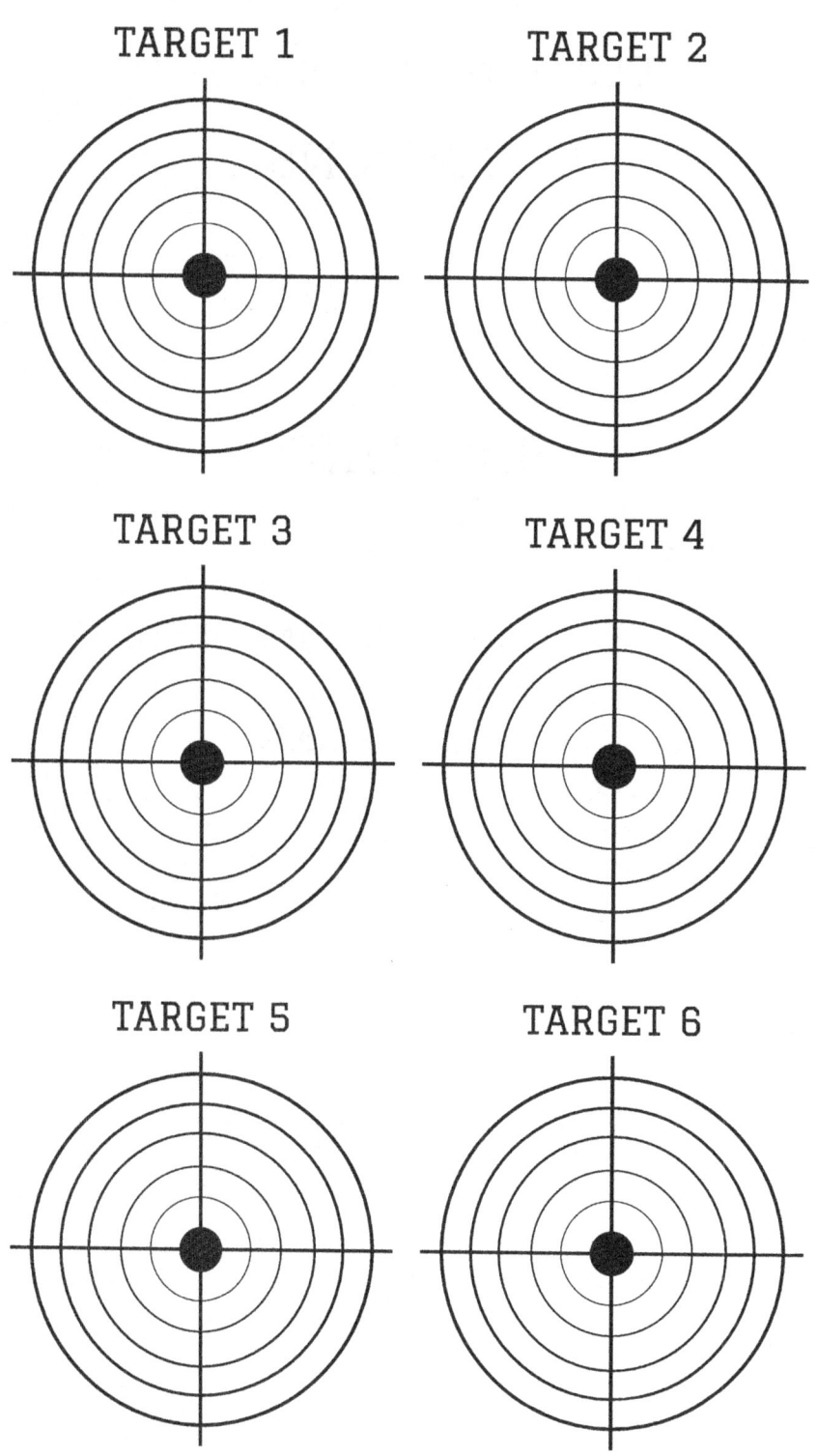

DATE / LOCATION: _____

CONDITIONS

WEATHER:

WIND:

SHOOTING

FIREARM:

BULLET: SEATING DEPTH:

POWDER: GRAINS:

PRIMER:

BRASS:

DISTANCE:

OVERALL RESULTS

★ ★ ★ ★ ★

NOTES

_____

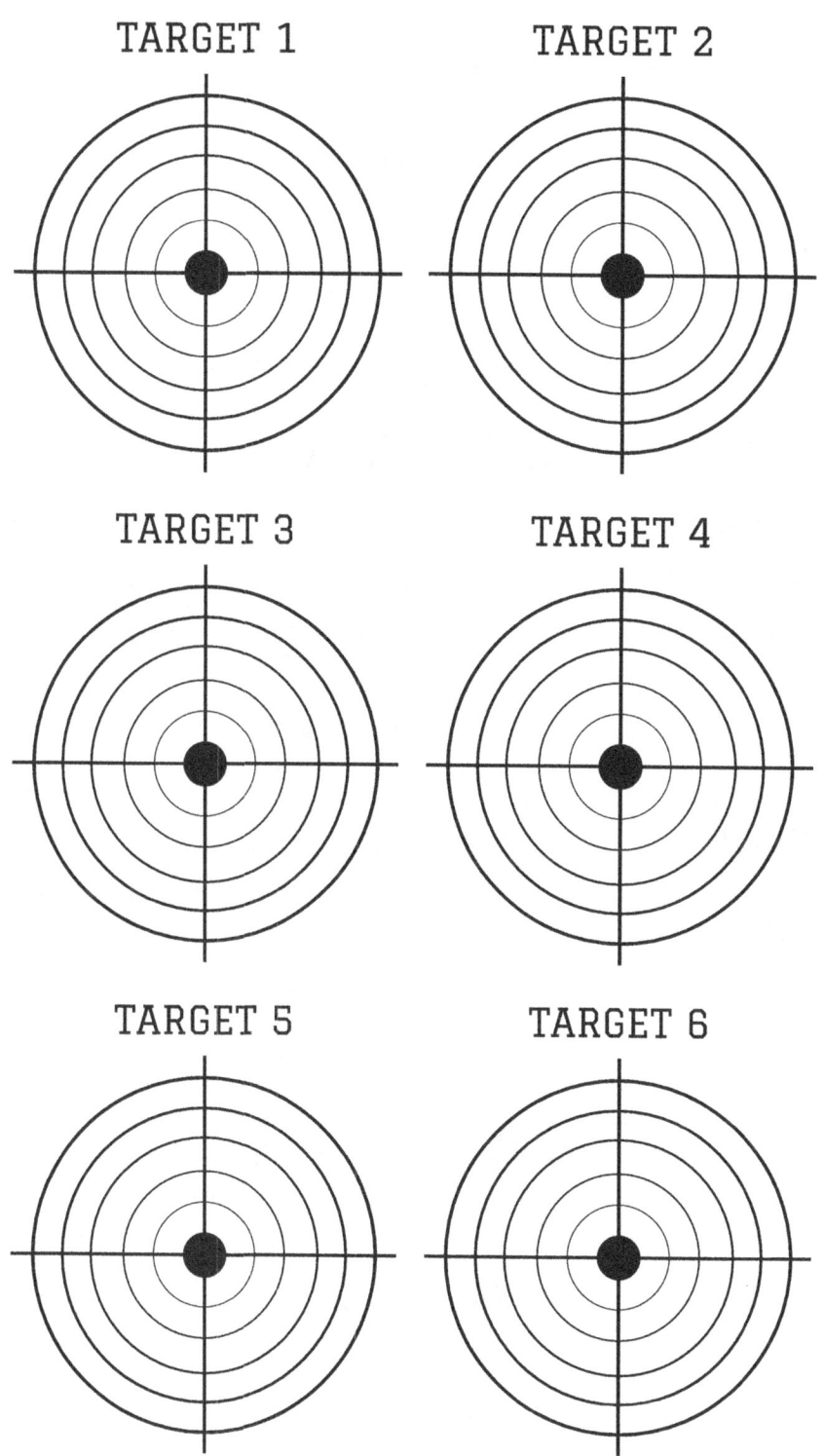

DATE / LOCATION: _____

CONDITIONS

WEATHER:

WIND:

SHOOTING

FIREARM:

BULLET: SEATING DEPTH:

POWDER: GRAINS:

PRIMER:

BRASS:

DISTANCE:

OVERALL RESULTS

★ ★ ★ ★ ★

NOTES

_____

_____

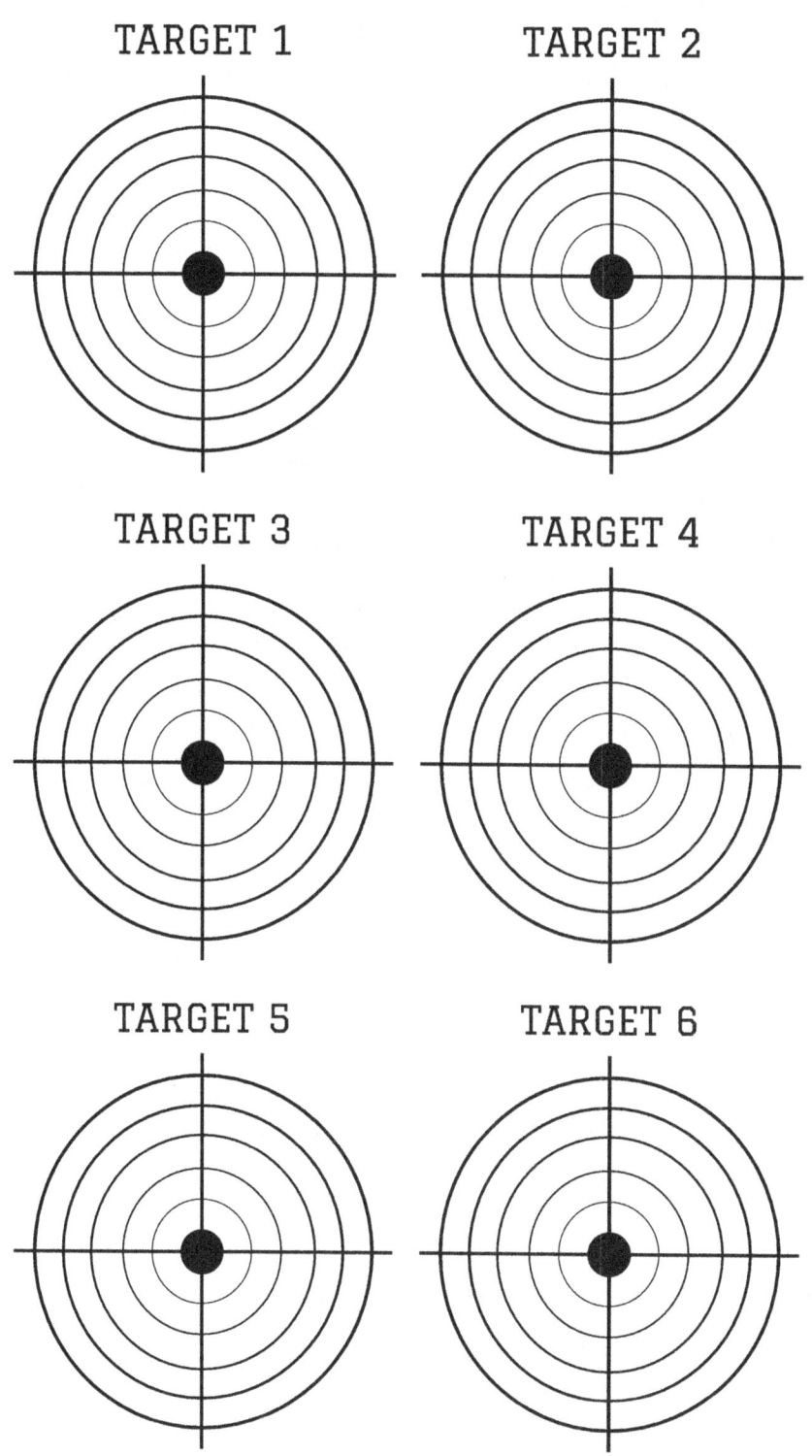

DATE / LOCATION: _____

CONDITIONS

WEATHER:

WIND:

SHOOTING

FIREARM:

| BULLET: | SEATING DEPTH: |
| POWDER: | GRAINS: |

PRIMER:

BRASS:

DISTANCE:

OVERALL RESULTS

★ ★ ★ ★ ★

NOTES

_____

_____

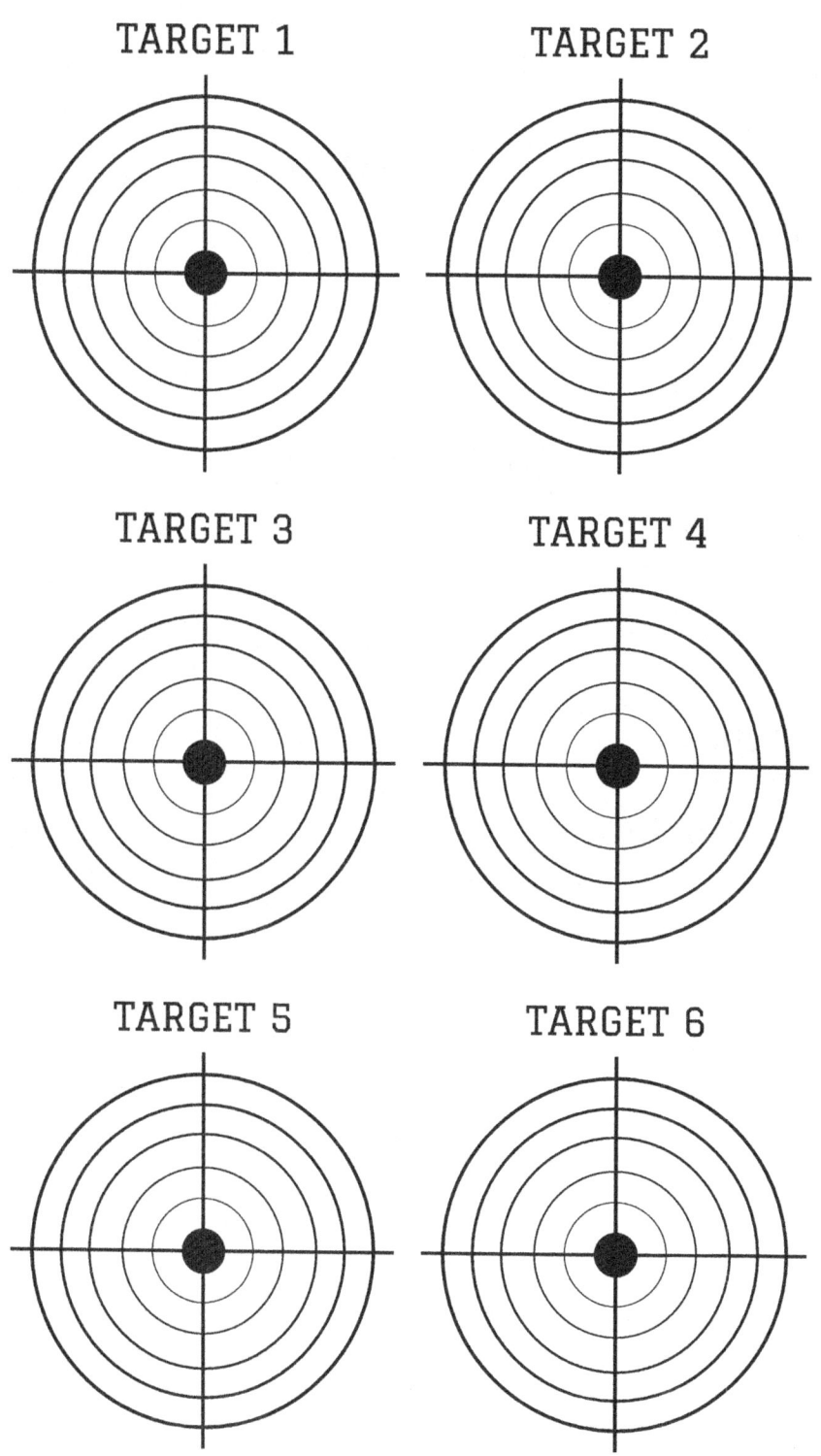

DATE / LOCATION: _____

CONDITIONS

WEATHER:

WIND:

SHOOTING

FIREARM:

BULLET: SEATING DEPTH:

POWDER: GRAINS:

PRIMER:

BRASS:

DISTANCE:

OVERALL RESULTS
★ ★ ★ ★ ★

NOTES

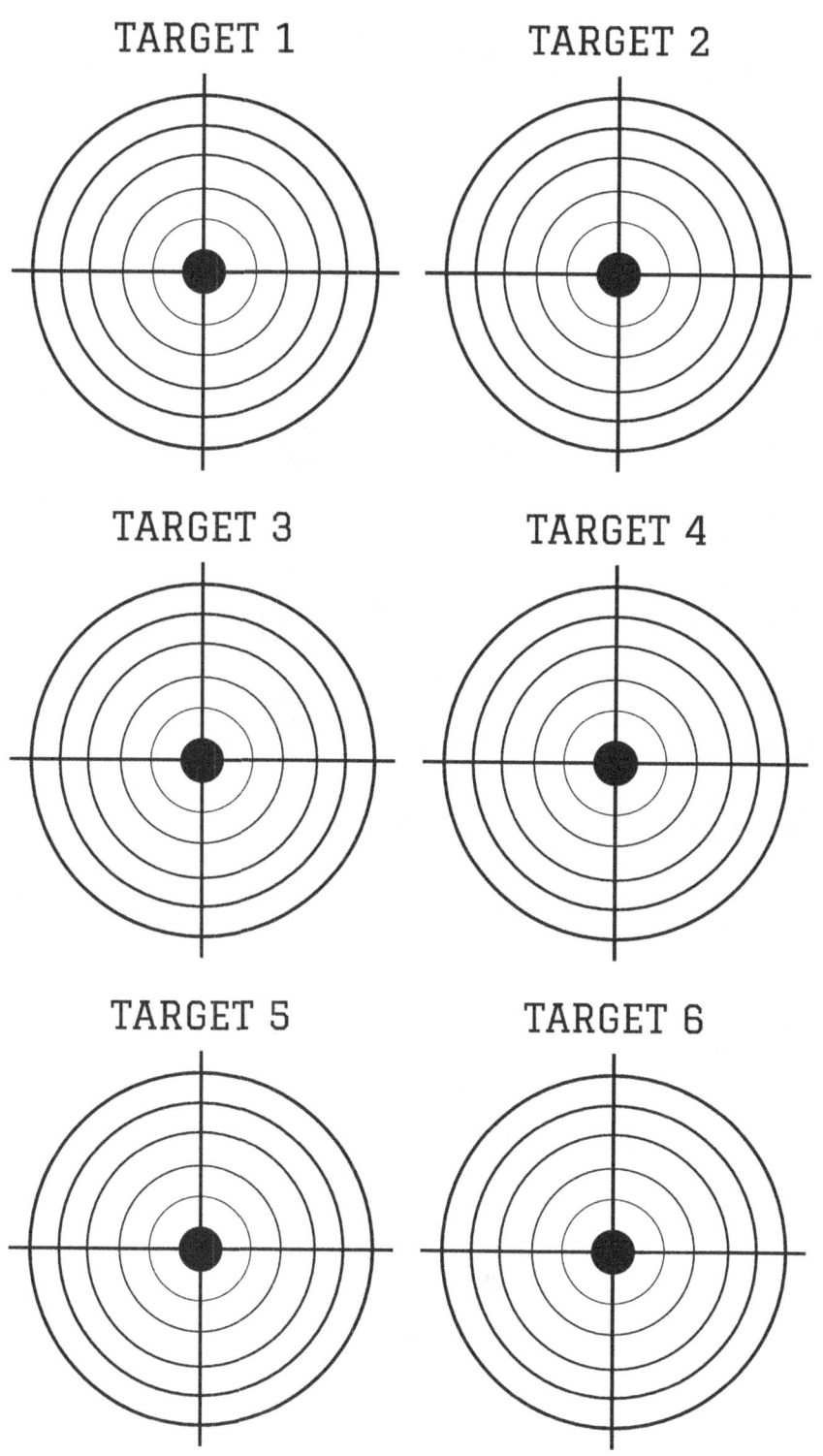

DATE / LOCATION: _____

CONDITIONS

WEATHER:

WIND:

SHOOTING

FIREARM:

BULLET: SEATING DEPTH:

POWDER: GRAINS:

PRIMER:

BRASS:

DISTANCE:

OVERALL RESULTS

☆ ☆ ☆ ☆ ☆

NOTES

_____

_____

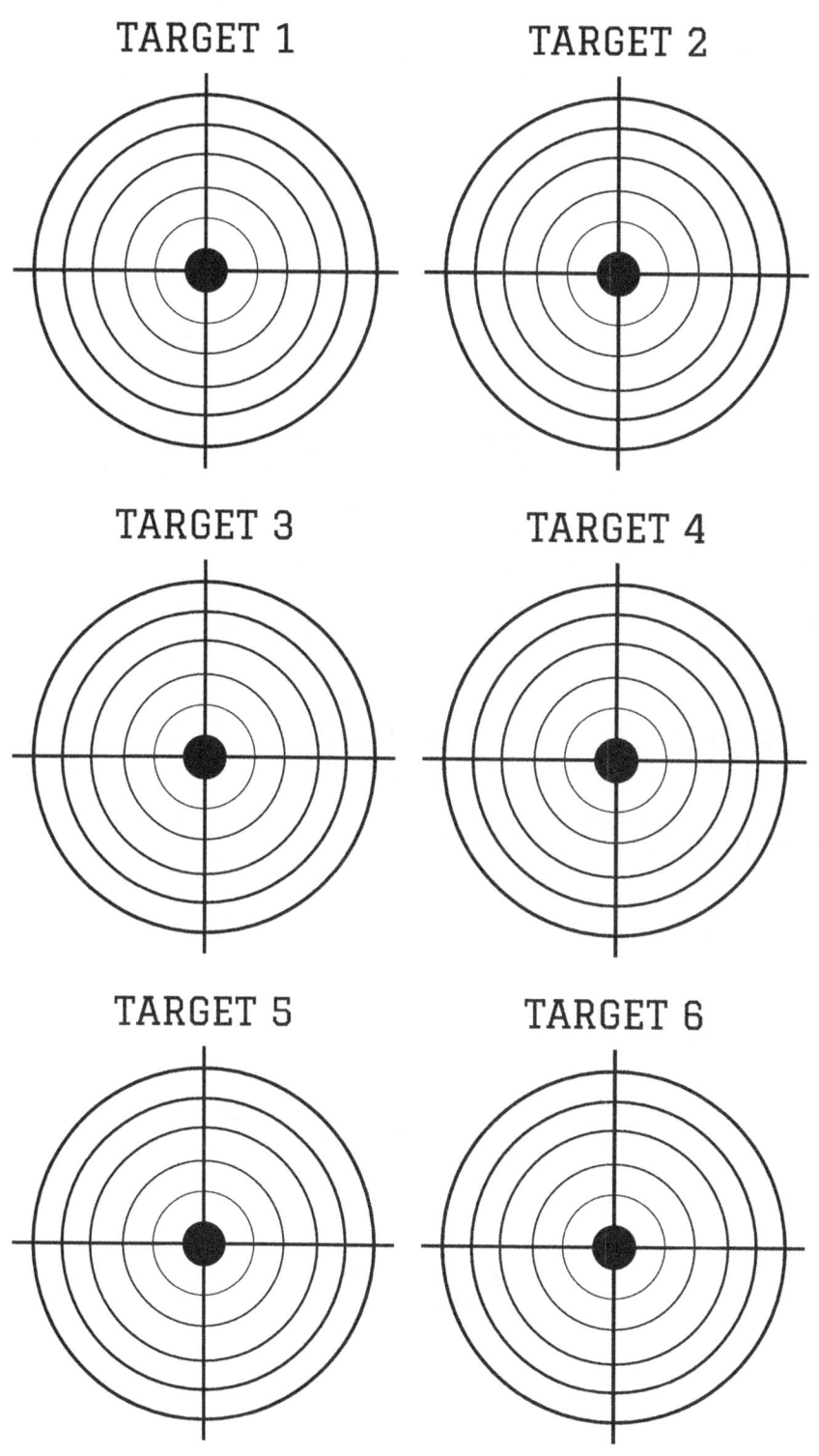

DATE / LOCATION: _____

CONDITIONS

WEATHER:

WIND:

SHOOTING

FIREARM:

BULLET: SEATING DEPTH:

POWDER: GRAINS:

PRIMER:

BRASS:

DISTANCE:

OVERALL RESULTS

★ ★ ★ ★ ★

NOTES

_____

_____

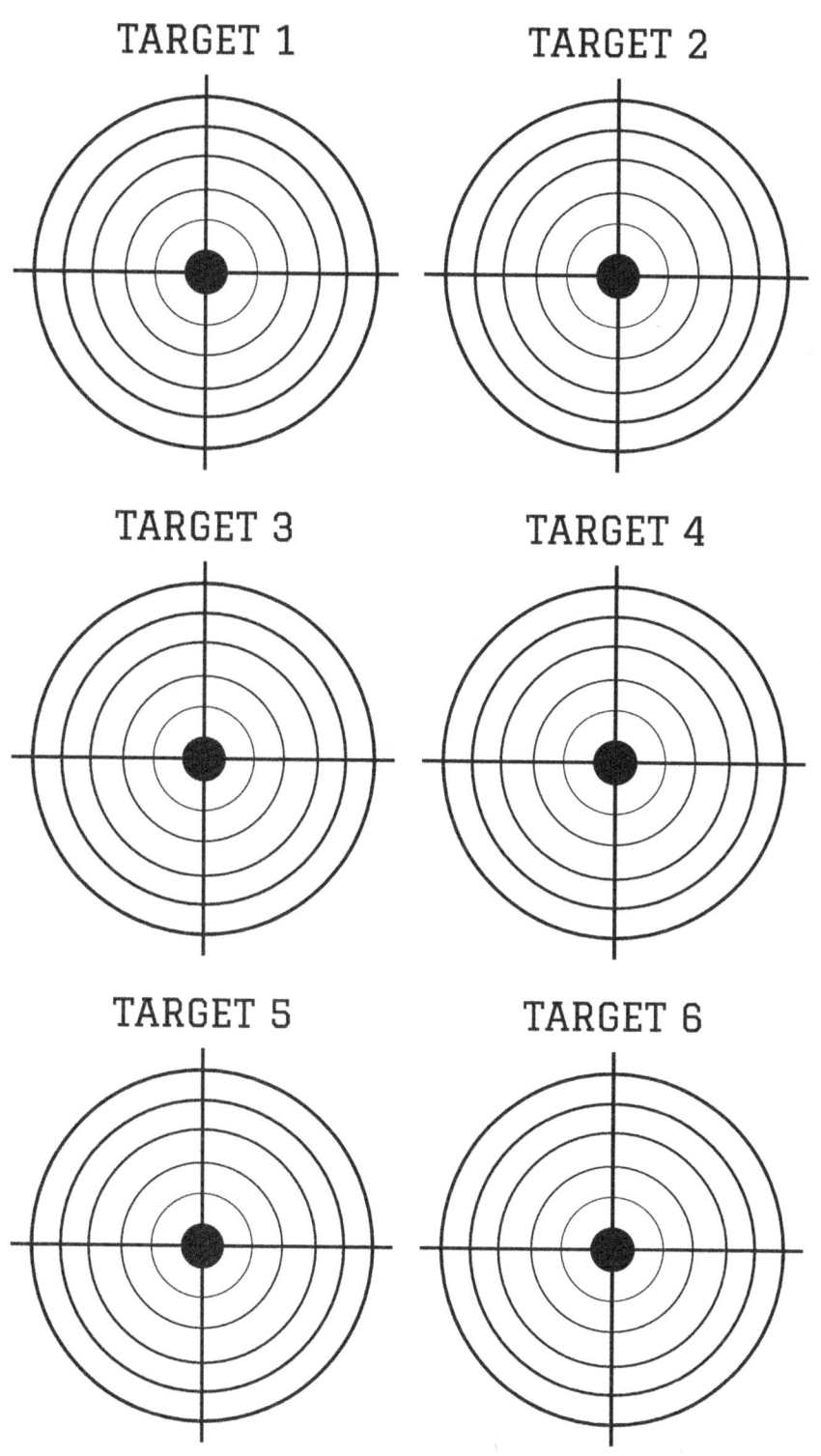

DATE / LOCATION: _____

CONDITIONS

WEATHER:

WIND:

SHOOTING

FIREARM:

BULLET:

SEATING DEPTH:

POWDER:

GRAINS:

PRIMER:

BRASS:

DISTANCE:

OVERALL RESULTS

★ ★ ★ ★ ★

NOTES

_____

_____

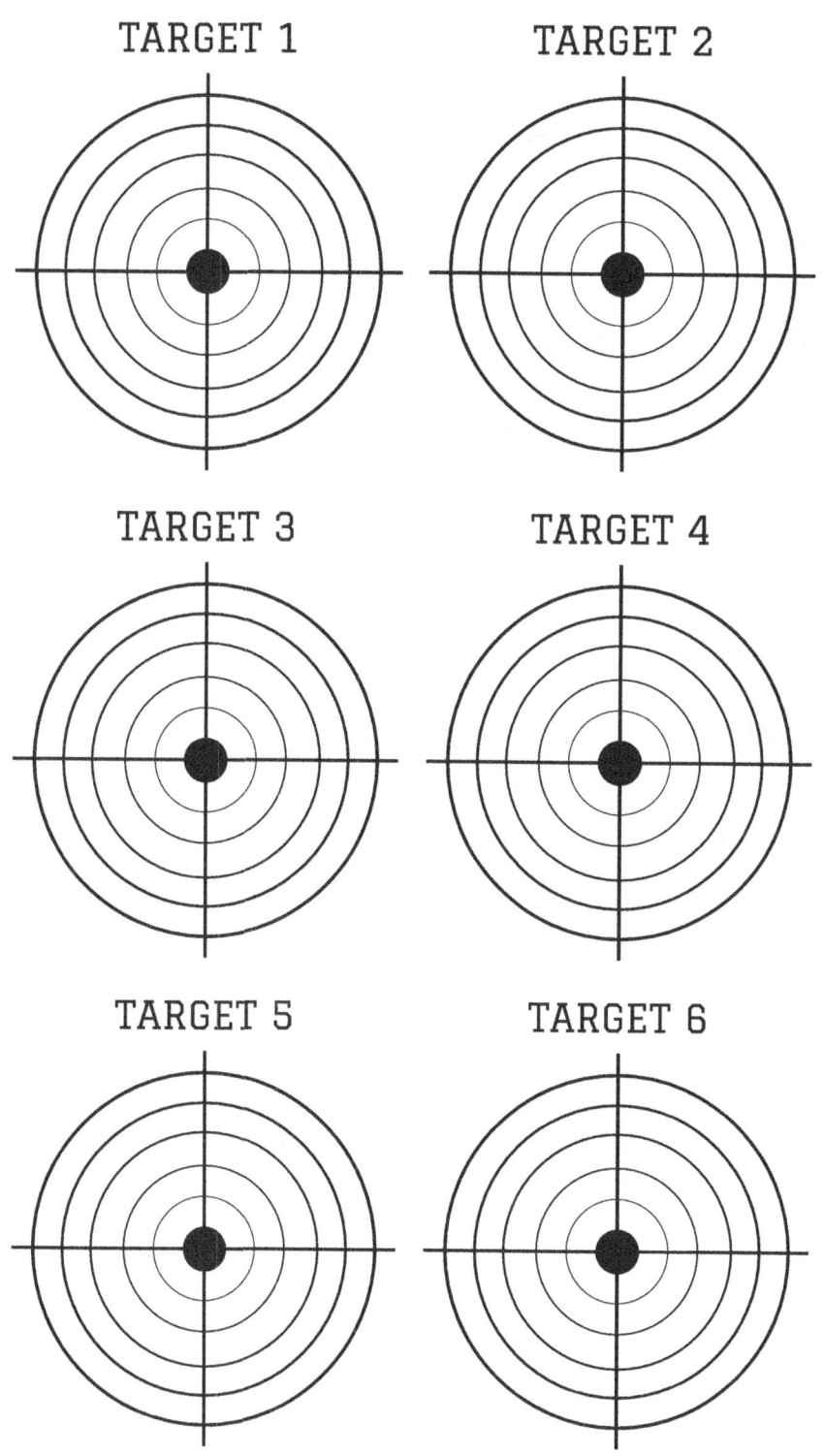

DATE / LOCATION: _____

CONDITIONS

WEATHER:

WIND:

SHOOTING

FIREARM:

BULLET: SEATING DEPTH:

POWDER: GRAINS:

PRIMER:

BRASS:

DISTANCE:

OVERALL RESULTS

★ ★ ★ ★ ★

NOTES

_____

_____

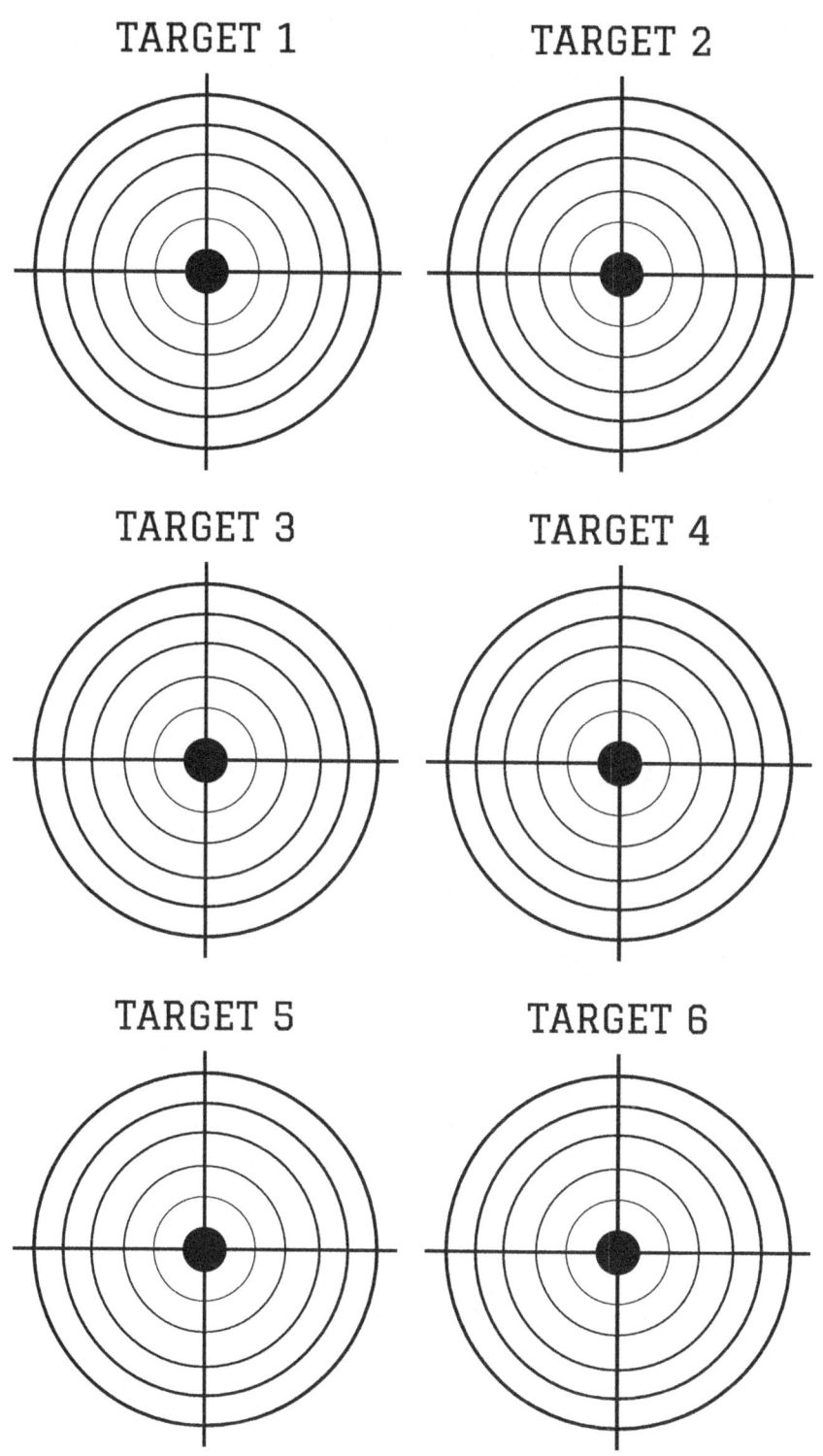

DATE / LOCATION: _____

CONDITIONS

WEATHER:

WIND:

SHOOTING

FIREARM:

BULLET: SEATING DEPTH:

POWDER: GRAINS:

PRIMER:

BRASS:

DISTANCE:

OVERALL RESULTS

★ ★ ★ ★ ★

NOTES

_____
_____

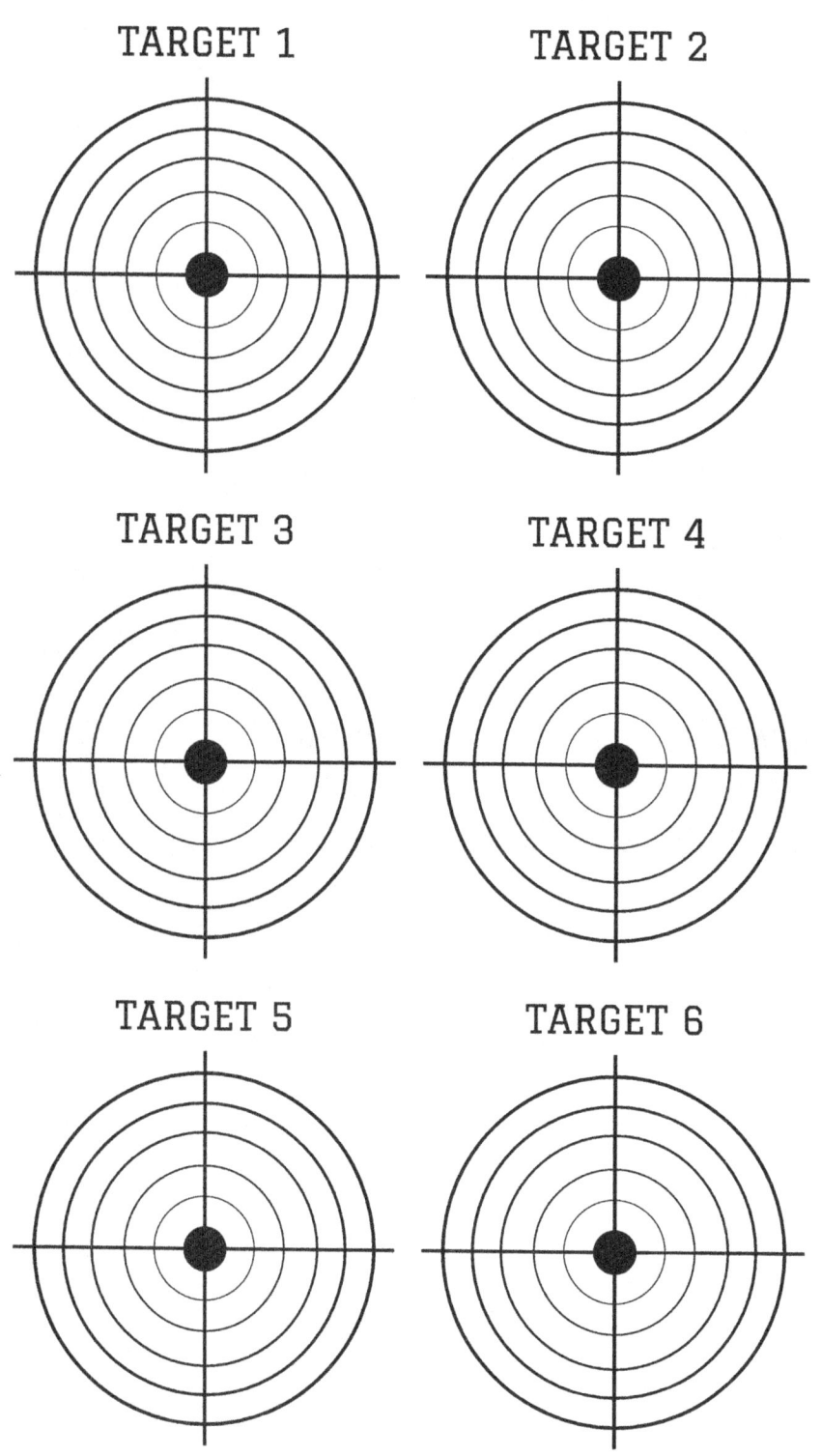

DATE / LOCATION: _____

CONDITIONS

WEATHER:

WIND:

SHOOTING

FIREARM:

BULLET: SEATING DEPTH:

POWDER: GRAINS:

PRIMER:

BRASS:

DISTANCE:

OVERALL RESULTS

☆ ☆ ☆ ☆ ☆

NOTES

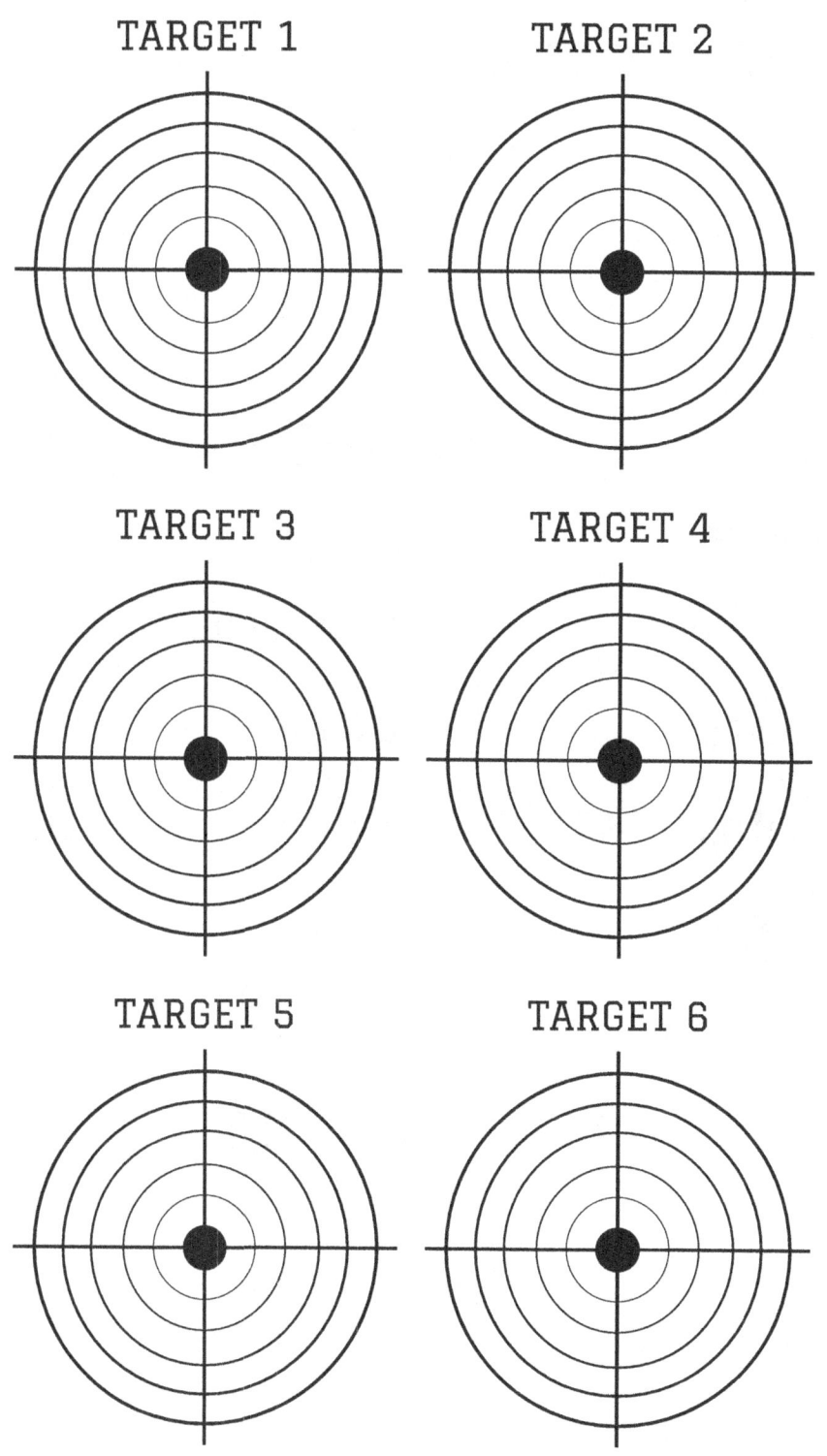

DATE / LOCATION: _____

CONDITIONS

WEATHER:

WIND:

SHOOTING

FIREARM:

BULLET:

SEATING DEPTH:

POWDER:

GRAINS:

PRIMER:

BRASS:

DISTANCE:

OVERALL RESULTS

☆ ☆ ☆ ☆ ☆

NOTES

_____

_____

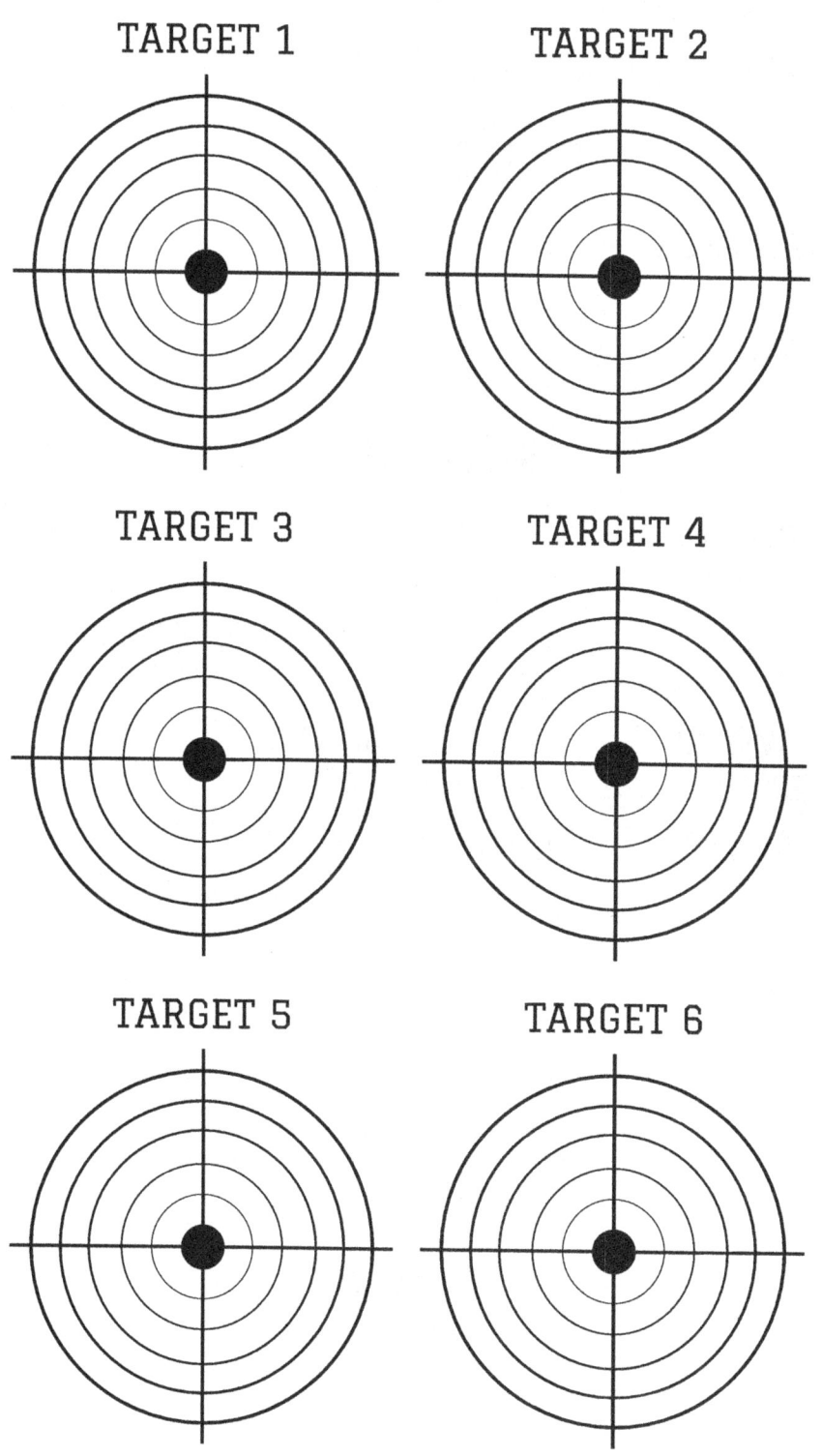

DATE / LOCATION: _____

CONDITIONS

WEATHER:

WIND:

SHOOTING

FIREARM:

BULLET: SEATING DEPTH:

POWDER: GRAINS:

PRIMER:

BRASS:

DISTANCE:

OVERALL RESULTS

☆ ☆ ☆ ☆ ☆

NOTES

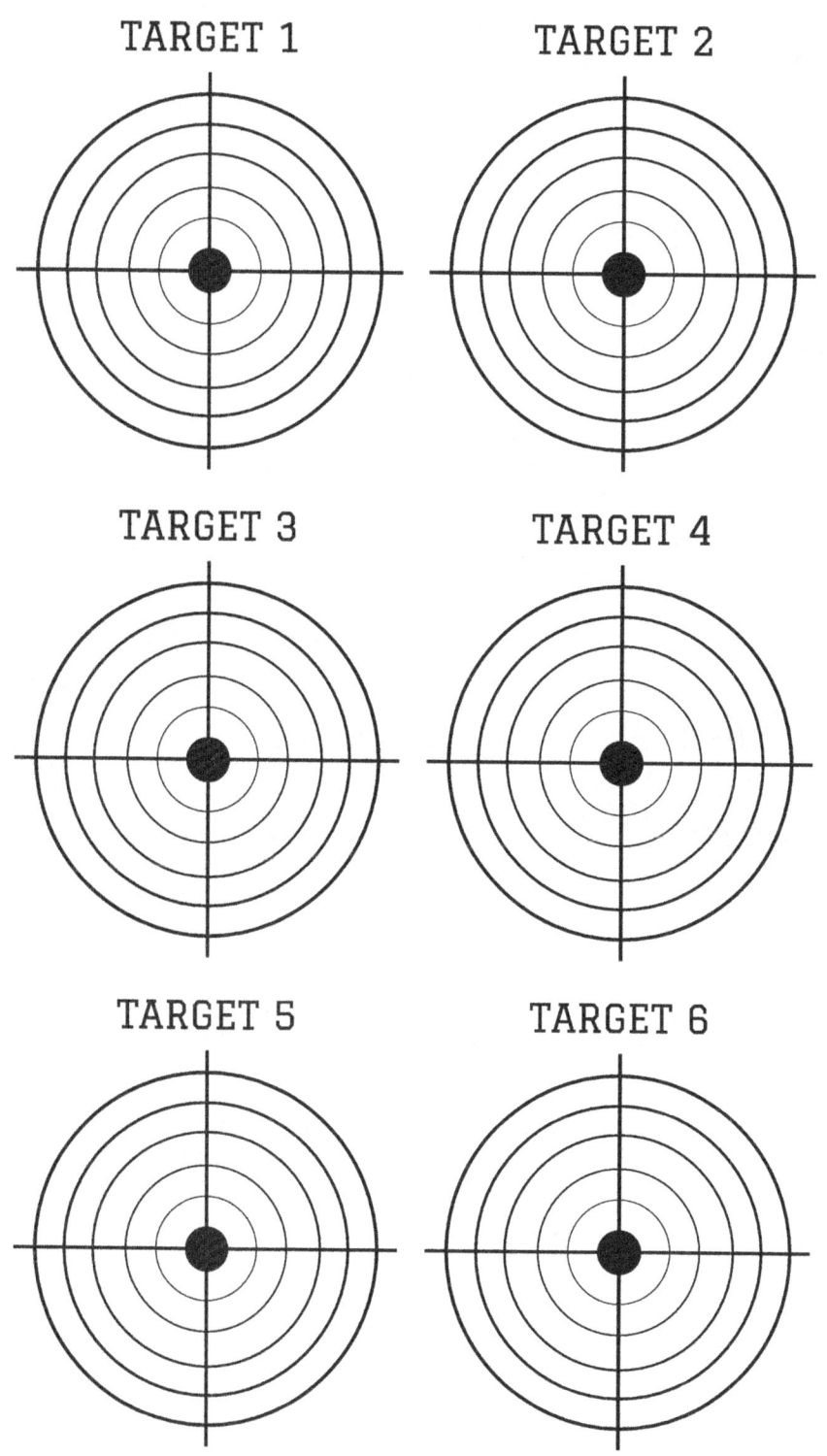

DATE / LOCATION: _____

CONDITIONS

WEATHER:

WIND:

SHOOTING

FIREARM:

BULLET: SEATING DEPTH:

POWDER: GRAINS:

PRIMER:

BRASS:

DISTANCE:

OVERALL RESULTS

★ ★ ★ ★ ★

NOTES

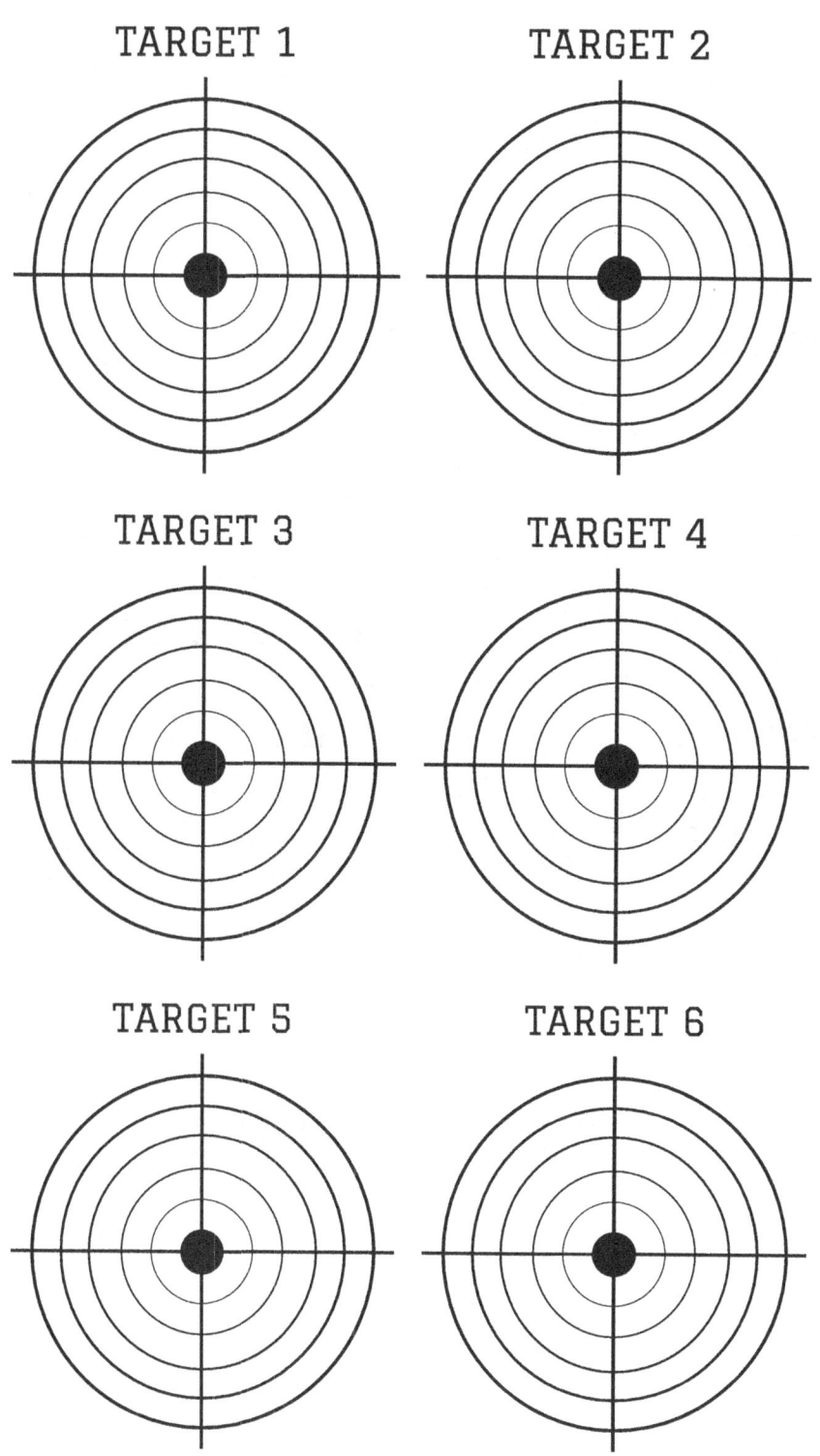

DATE / LOCATION: _____

CONDITIONS

WEATHER:

WIND:

SHOOTING

FIREARM:

BULLET:

SEATING DEPTH:

POWDER:

GRAINS:

PRIMER:

BRASS:

DISTANCE:

OVERALL RESULTS
★ ★ ★ ★ ★

NOTES

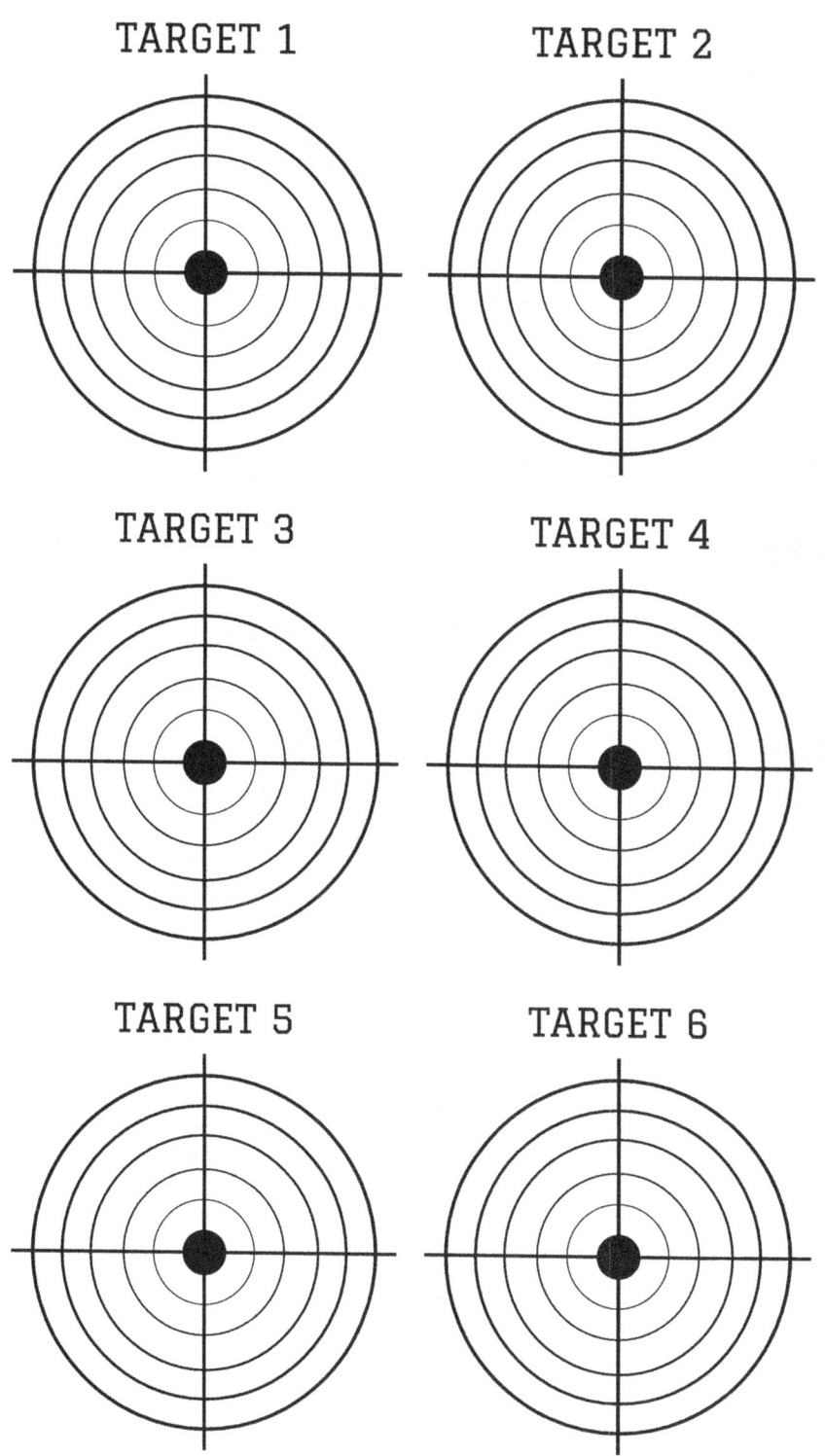

DATE / LOCATION: _____

CONDITIONS

WEATHER:

WIND:

SHOOTING

FIREARM:

BULLET: SEATING DEPTH:

POWDER: GRAINS:

PRIMER:

BRASS:

DISTANCE:

OVERALL RESULTS

★ ★ ★ ★ ★

NOTES

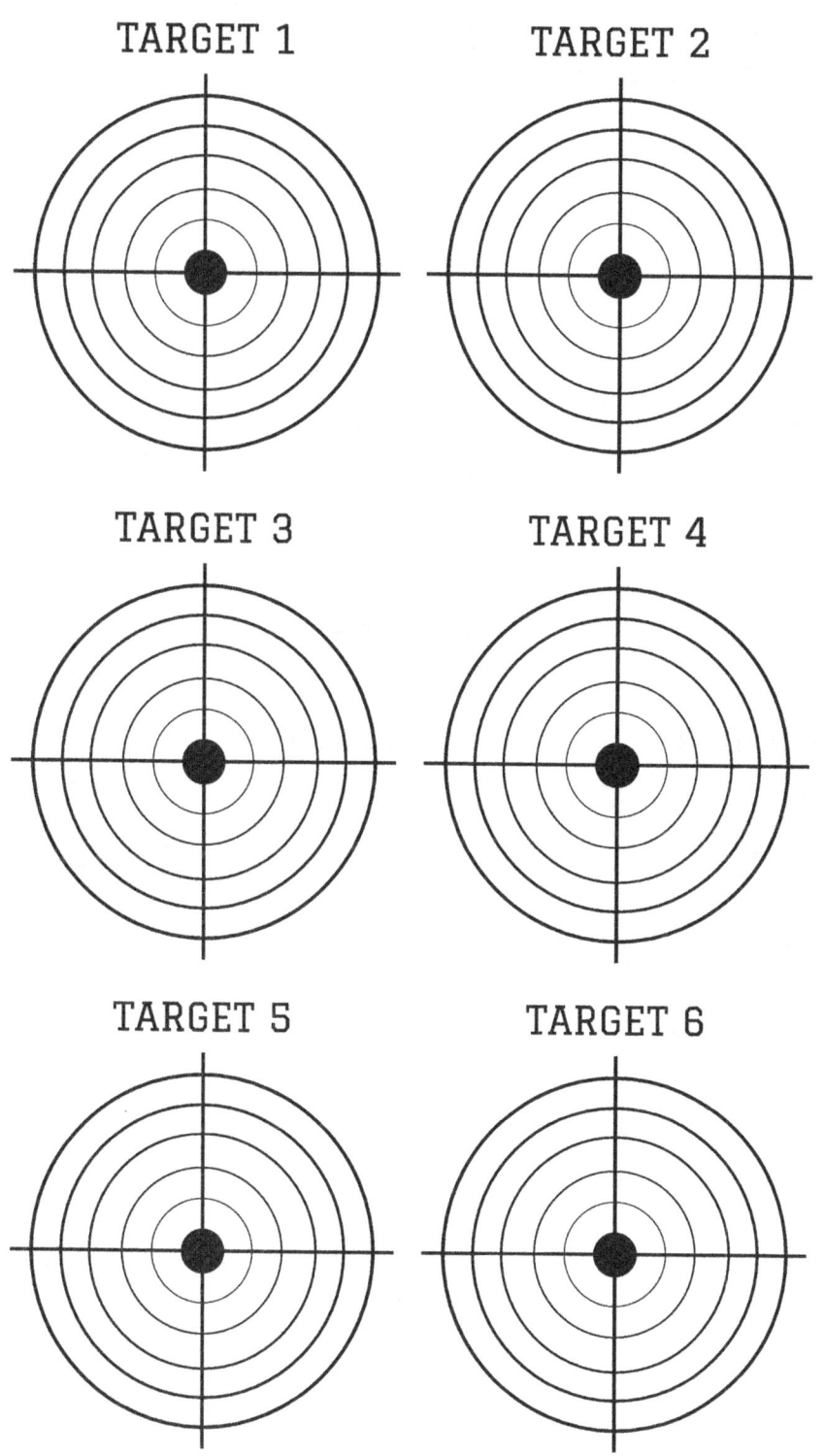

DATE / LOCATION: _____

CONDITIONS

WEATHER:

WIND:

SHOOTING

FIREARM:

BULLET: SEATING DEPTH:

POWDER: GRAINS:

PRIMER:

BRASS:

DISTANCE:

OVERALL RESULTS

★ ★ ★ ★ ★

NOTES

_____

_____

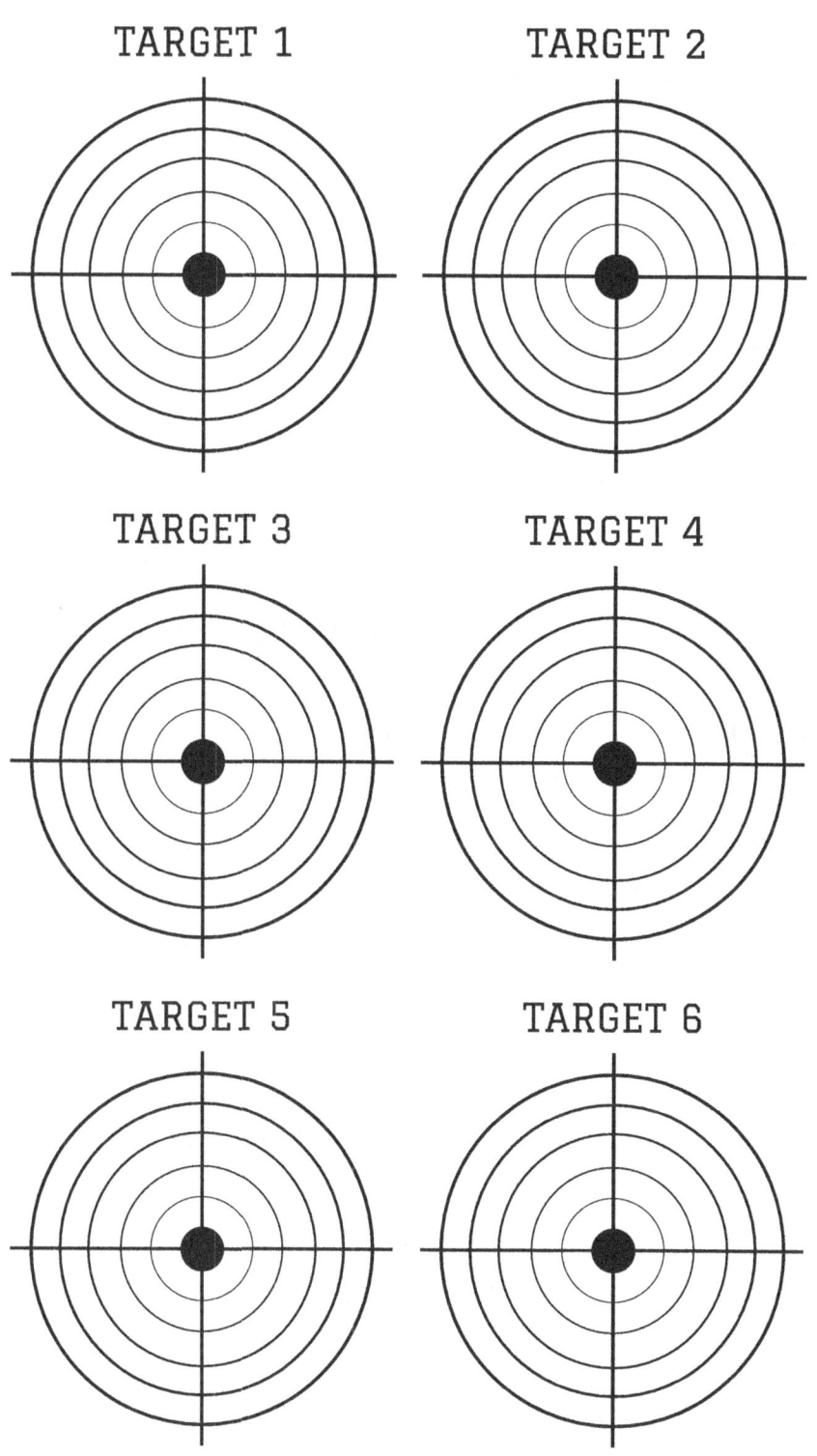

DATE / LOCATION: _____

CONDITIONS

WEATHER:

WIND:

SHOOTING

FIREARM:

BULLET:

SEATING DEPTH:

POWDER:

GRAINS:

PRIMER:

BRASS:

DISTANCE:

OVERALL RESULTS

★ ★ ★ ★ ★

NOTES

_____

_____

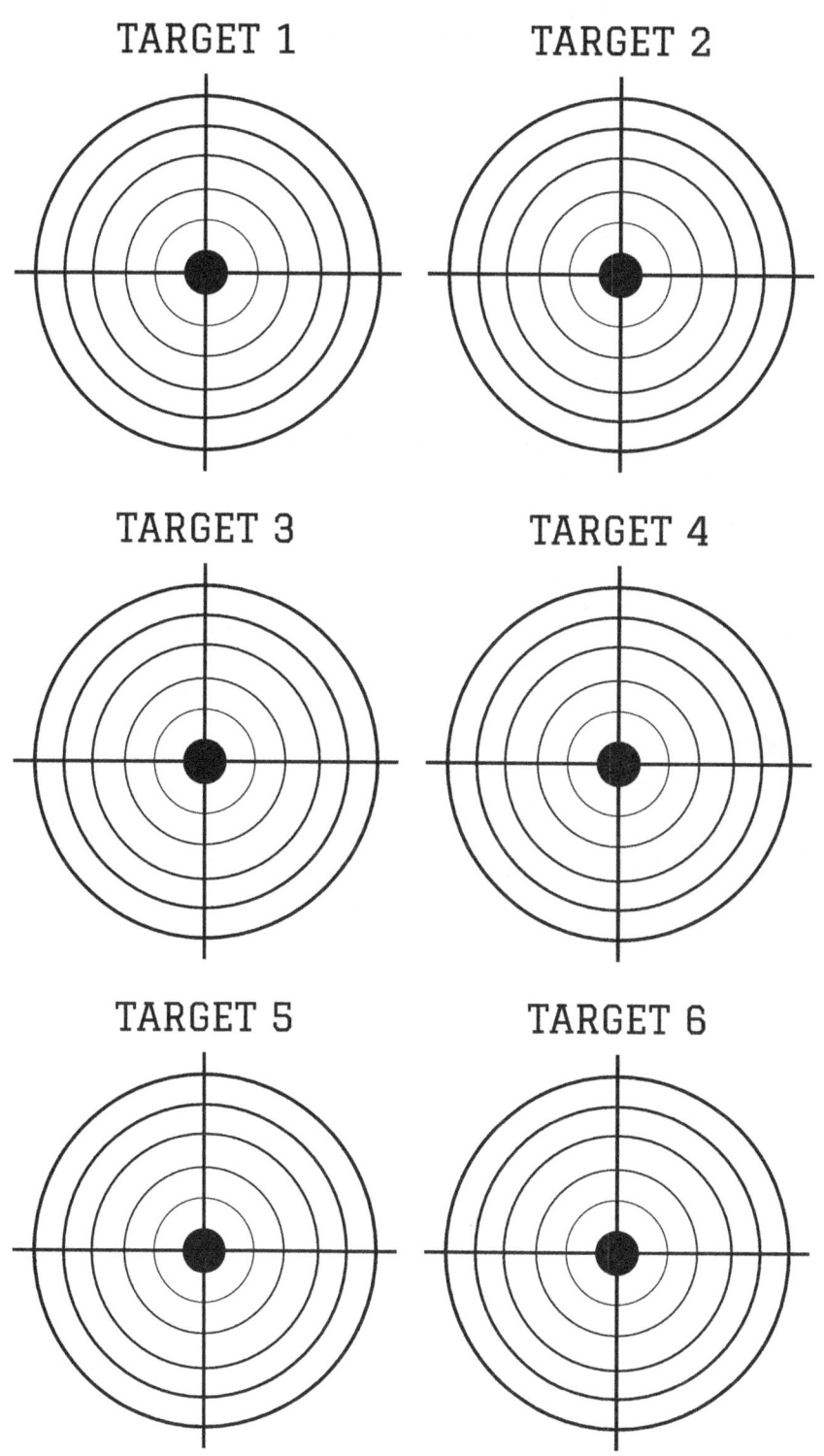

DATE / LOCATION: _____

CONDITIONS

WEATHER:

WIND:

SHOOTING

FIREARM:

BULLET: | SEATING DEPTH:

POWDER: | GRAINS:

PRIMER:

BRASS:

DISTANCE:

OVERALL RESULTS

★ ★ ★ ★ ★

NOTES

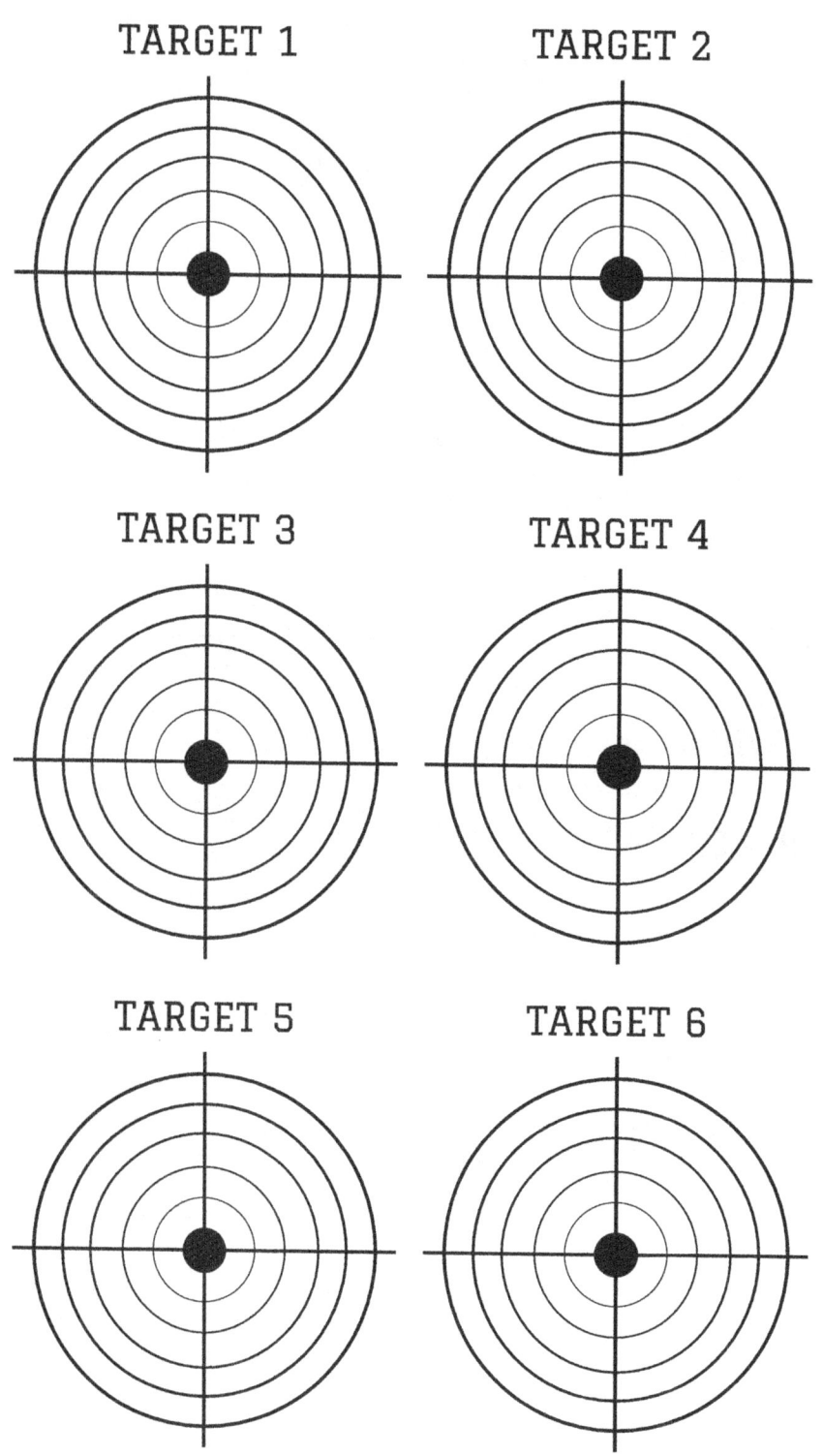

DATE / LOCATION: _____

CONDITIONS

WEATHER:

WIND:

SHOOTING

FIREARM:

BULLET: SEATING DEPTH:

POWDER: GRAINS:

PRIMER:

BRASS:

DISTANCE:

OVERALL RESULTS

★ ★ ★ ★ ★

NOTES

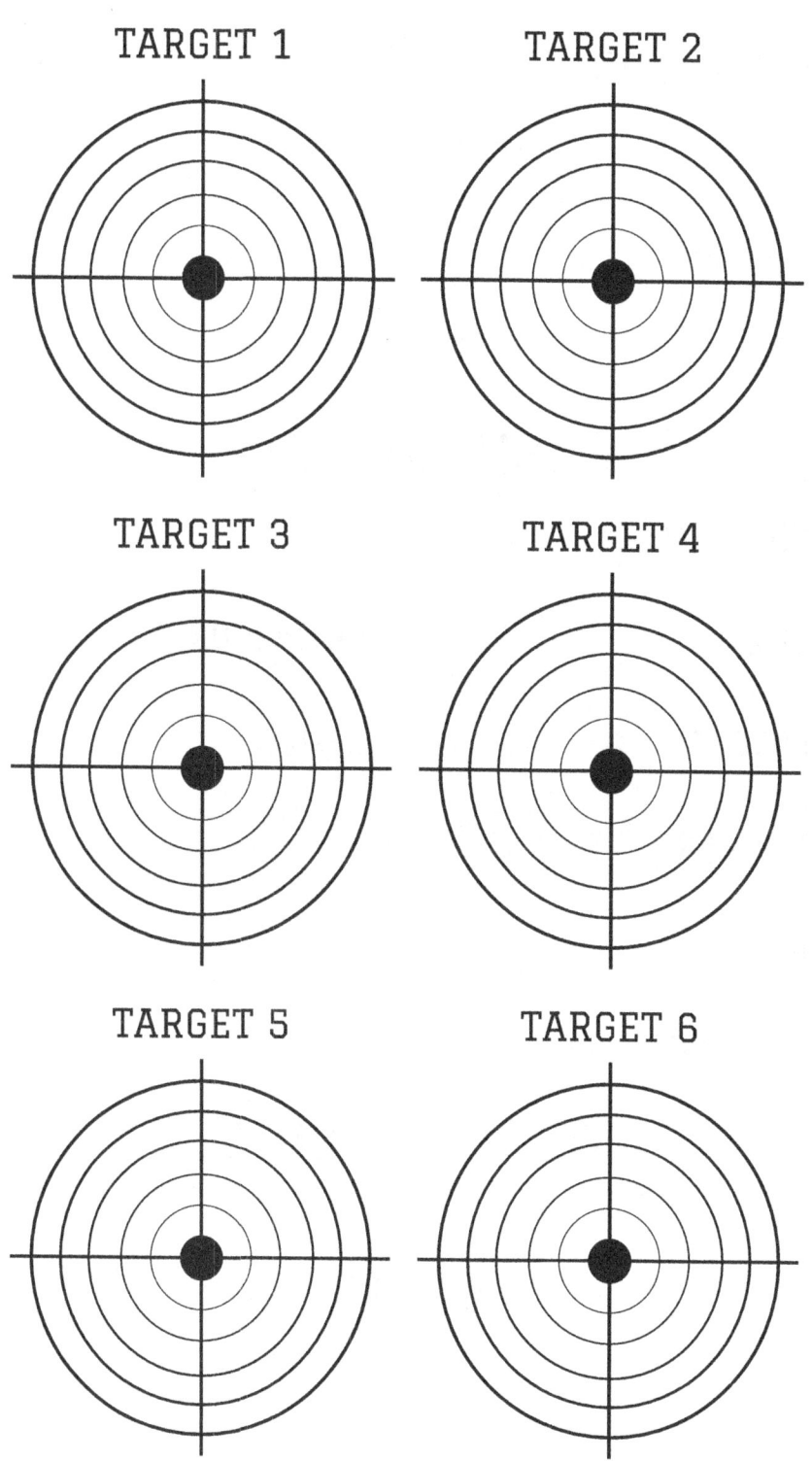

DATE / LOCATION: _____

CONDITIONS

WEATHER:

WIND:

SHOOTING

FIREARM:

BULLET: SEATING DEPTH:

POWDER: GRAINS:

PRIMER:

BRASS:

DISTANCE:

OVERALL RESULTS
★ ★ ★ ★ ★

NOTES

_____

_____

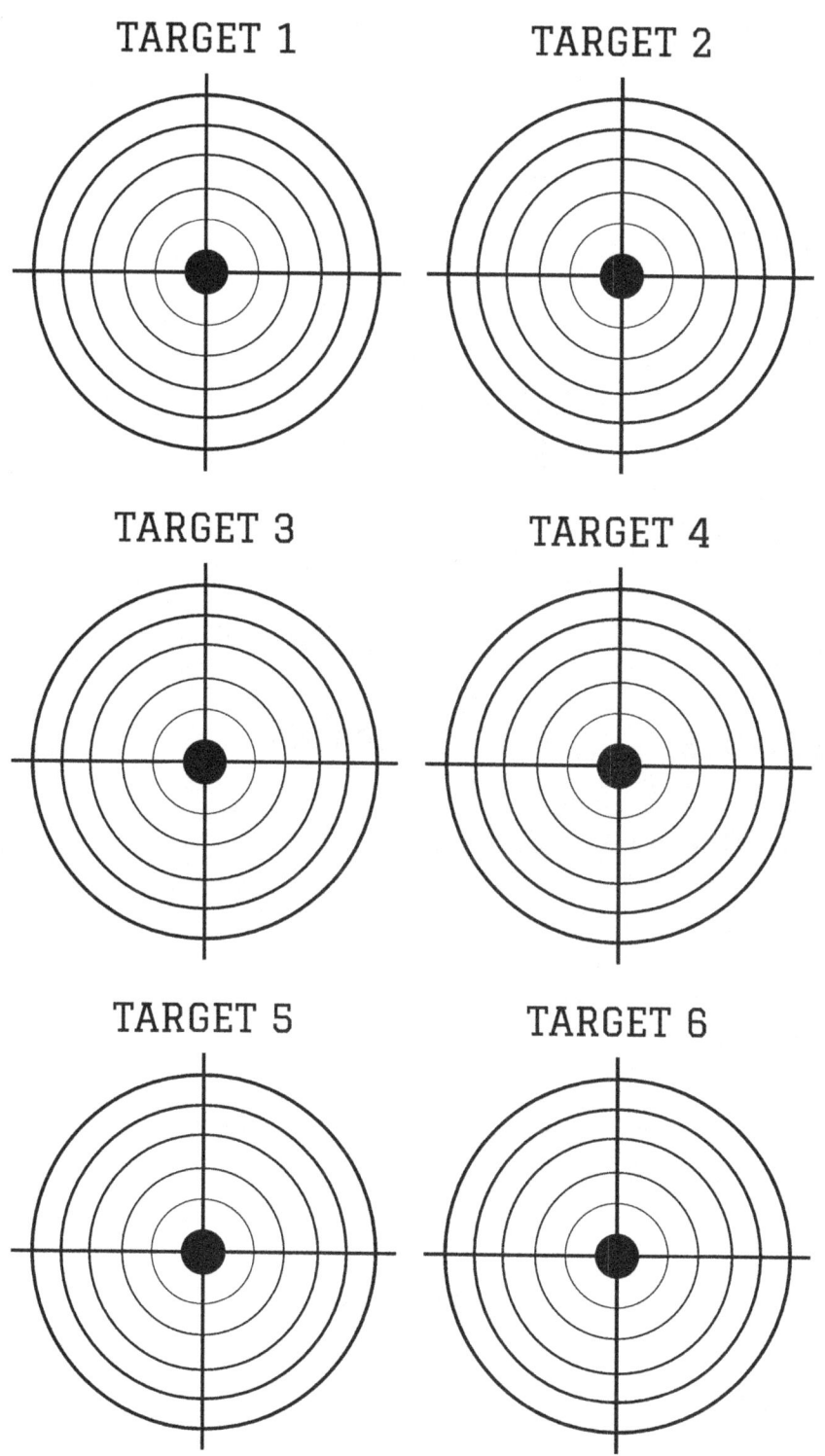

DATE / LOCATION: _____

CONDITIONS

WEATHER:

WIND:

SHOOTING

FIREARM:

BULLET:

SEATING DEPTH:

POWDER:

GRAINS:

PRIMER:

BRASS:

DISTANCE:

OVERALL RESULTS

★ ★ ★ ★ ★

NOTES

_____

_____

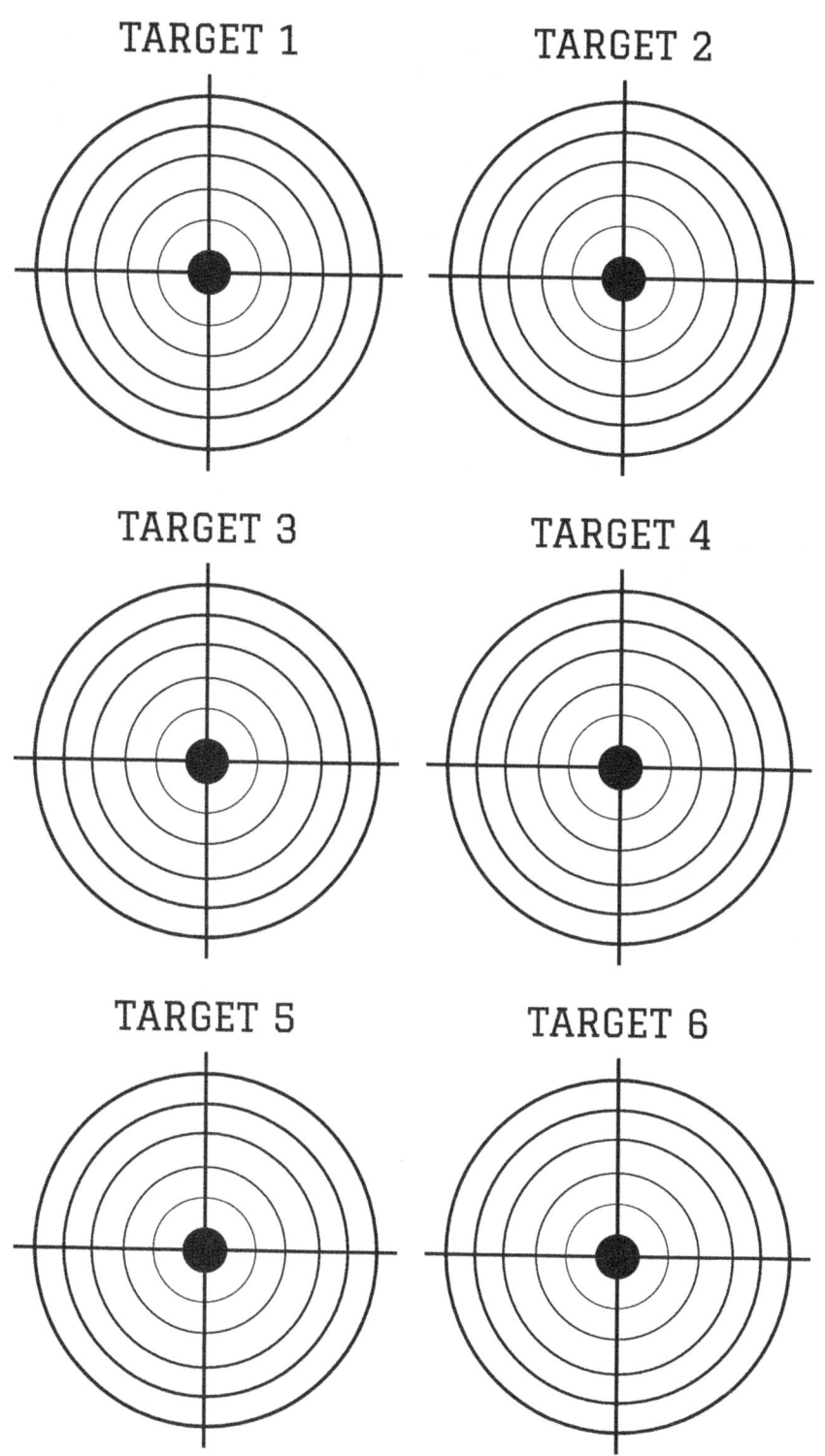

DATE / LOCATION: _____

CONDITIONS

WEATHER:

WIND:

SHOOTING

FIREARM:

BULLET:

SEATING DEPTH:

POWDER:

GRAINS:

PRIMER:

BRASS:

DISTANCE:

OVERALL RESULTS

★ ★ ★ ★ ★

NOTES

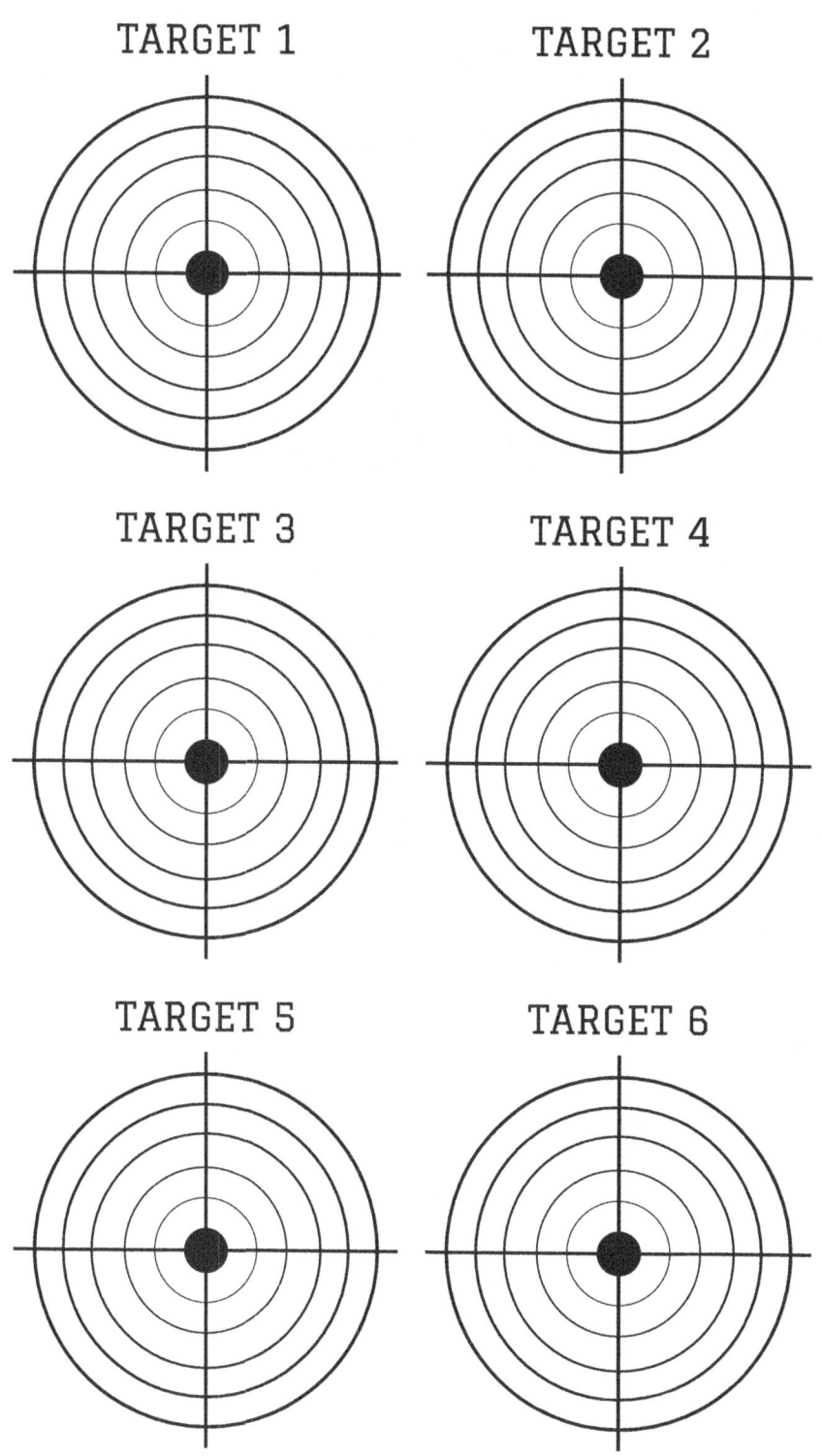

DATE / LOCATION: _____

CONDITIONS

WEATHER:

WIND:

SHOOTING

FIREARM:

BULLET: SEATING DEPTH:

POWDER: GRAINS:

PRIMER:

BRASS:

DISTANCE:

OVERALL RESULTS

★ ★ ★ ★ ★

NOTES

_____

_____

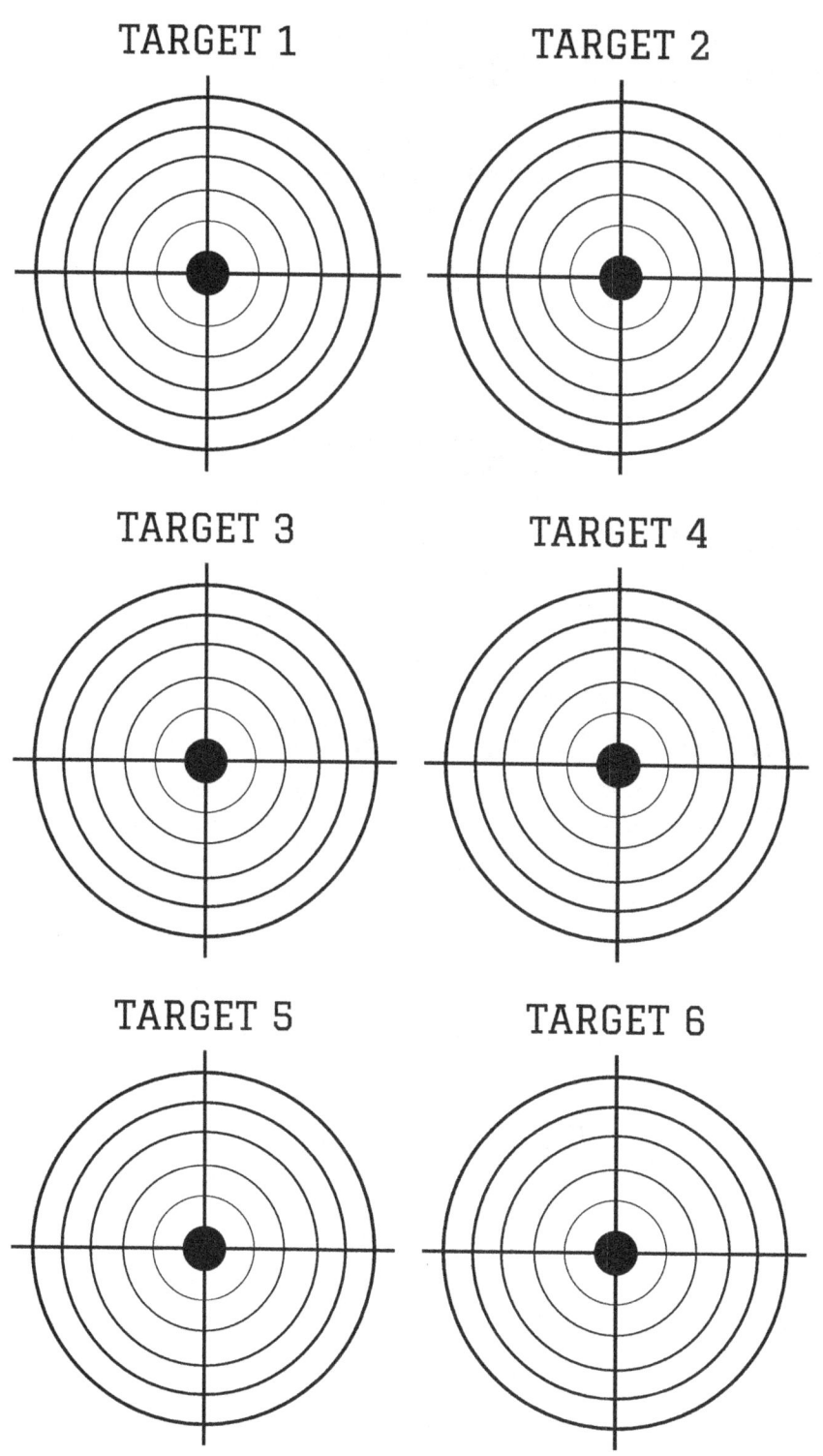

DATE / LOCATION: _____

CONDITIONS

WEATHER:

WIND:

SHOOTING

FIREARM:

BULLET: SEATING DEPTH:

POWDER: GRAINS:

PRIMER:

BRASS:

DISTANCE:

OVERALL RESULTS

★ ★ ★ ★ ★

NOTES

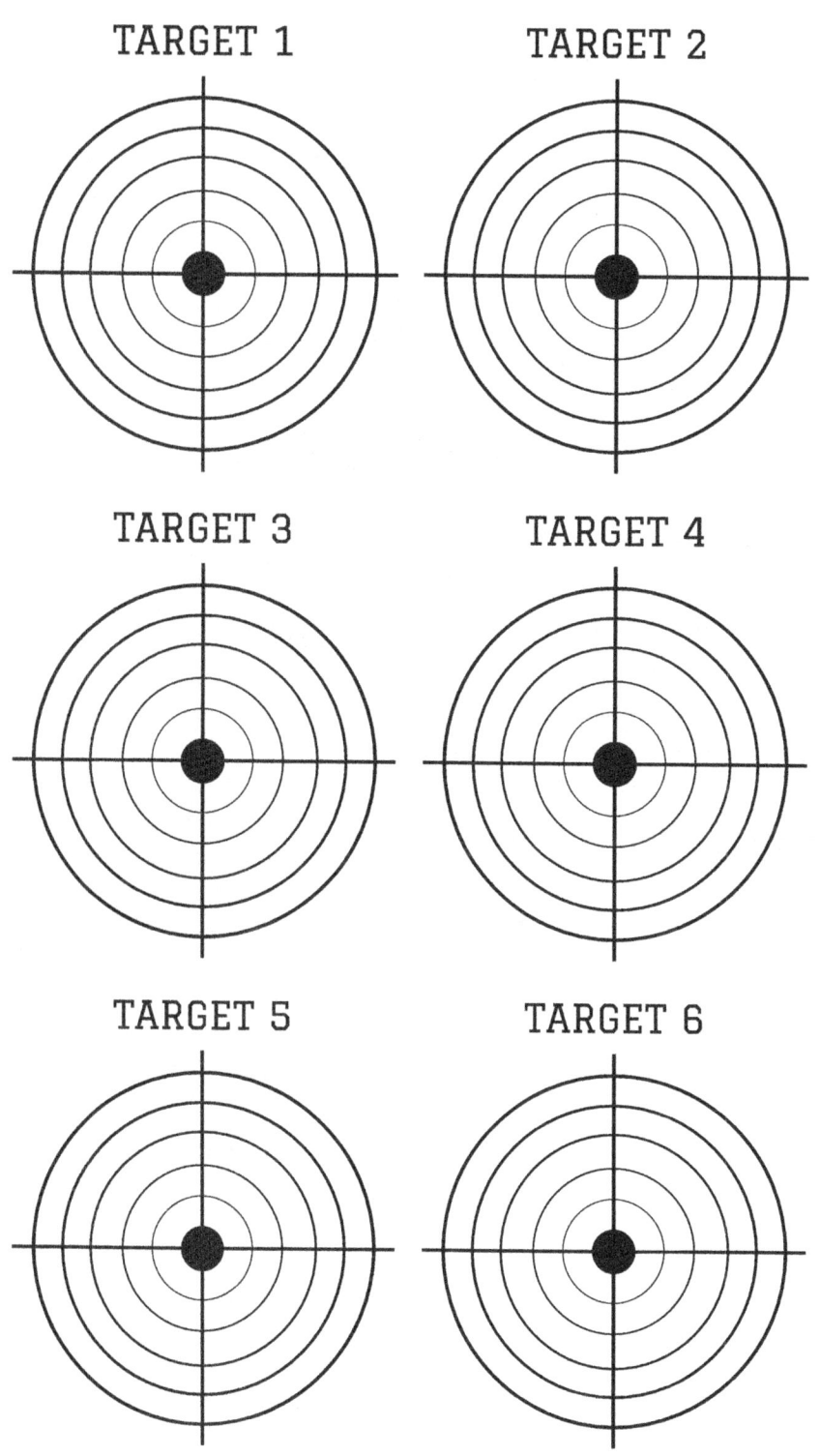

DATE / LOCATION: _____

CONDITIONS

WEATHER:

WIND:

SHOOTING

FIREARM:

BULLET:

SEATING DEPTH:

POWDER:

GRAINS:

PRIMER:

BRASS:

DISTANCE:

OVERALL RESULTS

★ ★ ★ ★ ★

NOTES

_____

_____

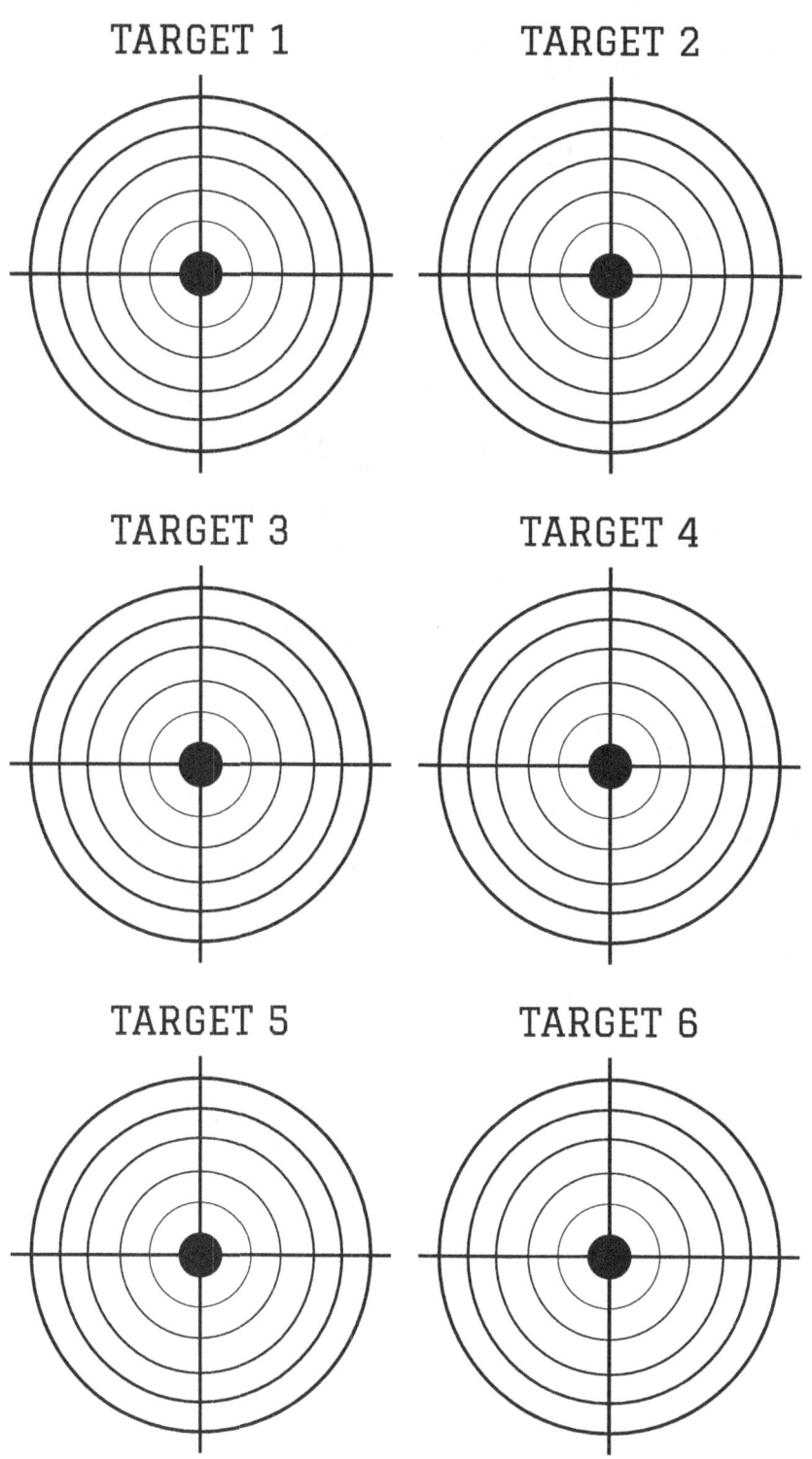

DATE / LOCATION: _____

CONDITIONS

WEATHER:

WIND:

SHOOTING

FIREARM:

BULLET: SEATING DEPTH:

POWDER: GRAINS:

PRIMER:

BRASS:

DISTANCE:

OVERALL RESULTS

★ ★ ★ ★ ★

NOTES

_____

_____

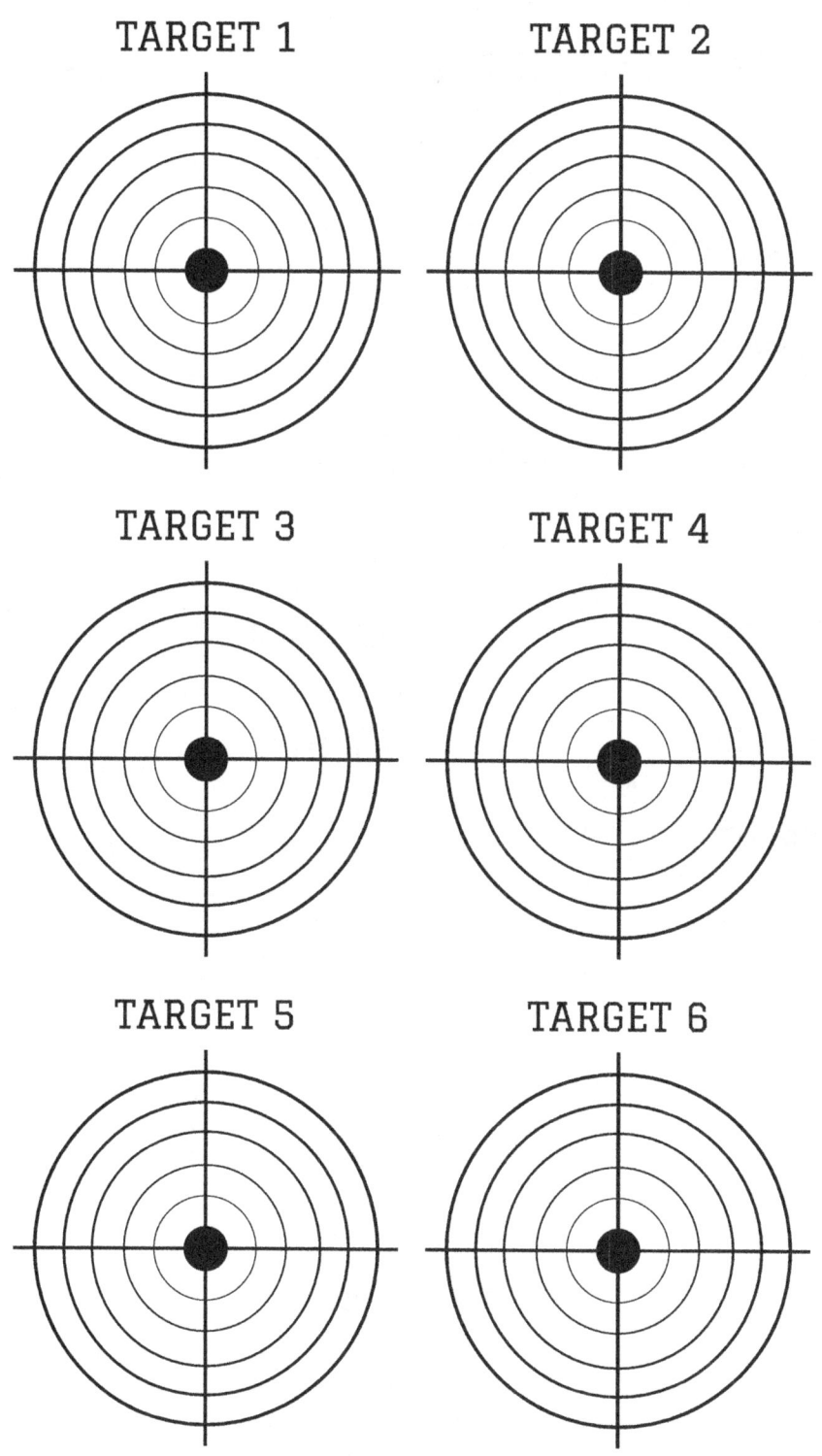

DATE / LOCATION: _____

CONDITIONS

WEATHER:

WIND:

SHOOTING

FIREARM:

BULLET:

SEATING DEPTH:

POWDER:

GRAINS:

PRIMER:

BRASS:

DISTANCE:

OVERALL RESULTS

☆ ☆ ☆ ☆ ☆

NOTES

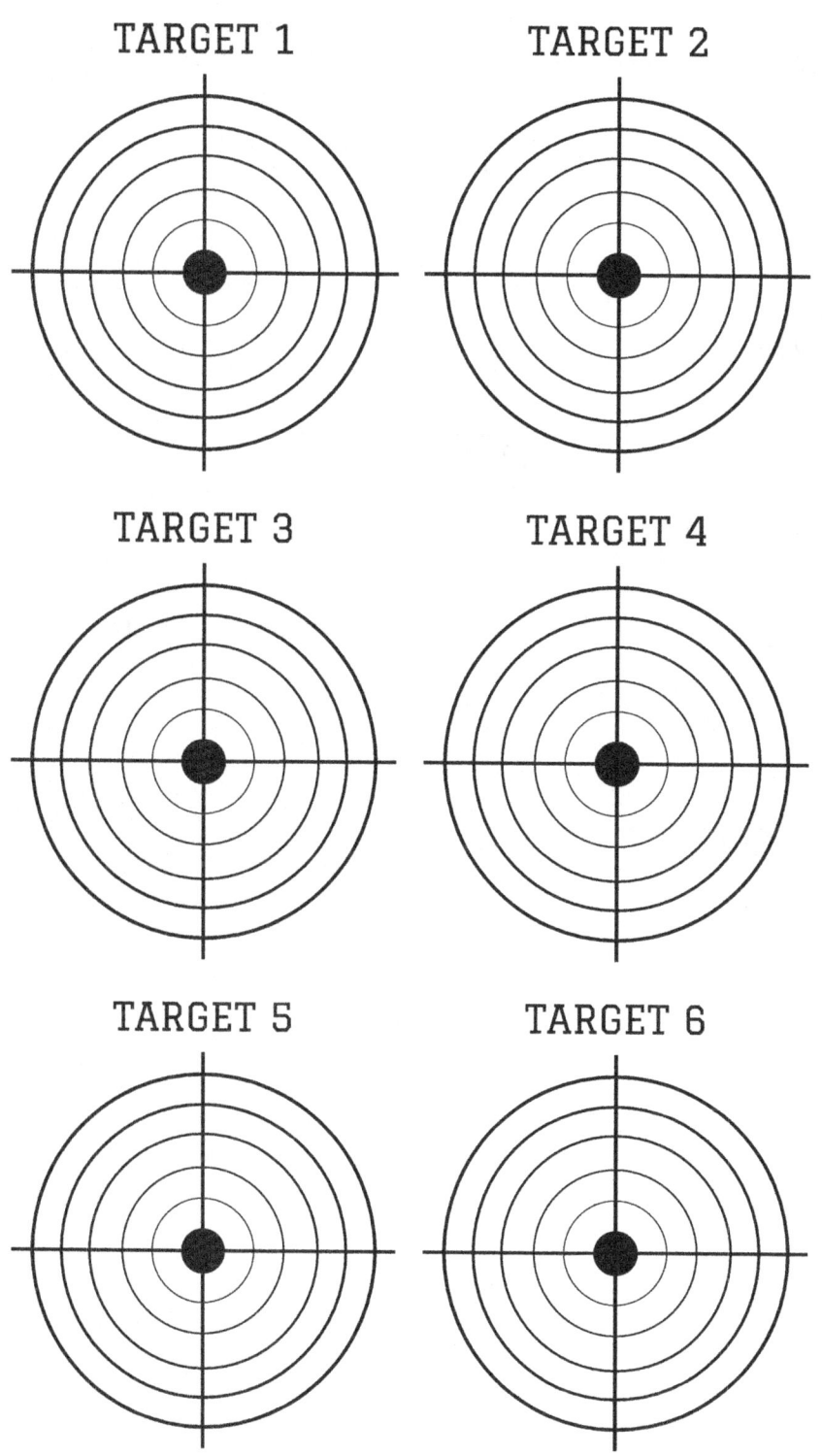

DATE / LOCATION: _____

CONDITIONS

WEATHER:

WIND:

SHOOTING

FIREARM:

BULLET: SEATING DEPTH:

POWDER: GRAINS:

PRIMER:

BRASS:

DISTANCE:

OVERALL RESULTS
☆ ☆ ☆ ☆ ☆

NOTES

_____

_____

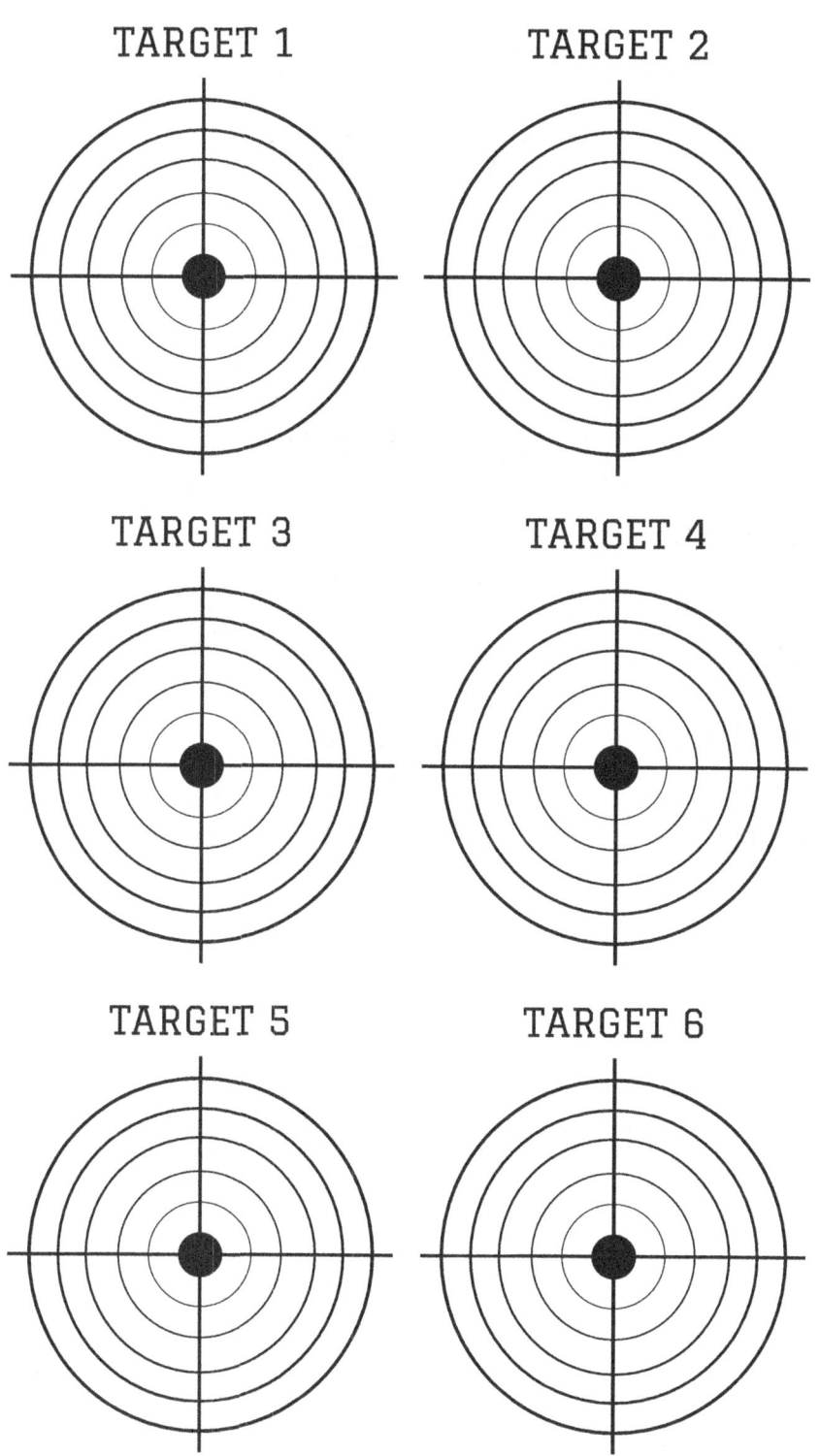

DATE / LOCATION: _____

CONDITIONS

WEATHER:

WIND:

SHOOTING

FIREARM:

BULLET:

SEATING DEPTH:

POWDER:

GRAINS:

PRIMER:

BRASS:

DISTANCE:

OVERALL RESULTS

★ ★ ★ ★ ★

NOTES

_____

_____

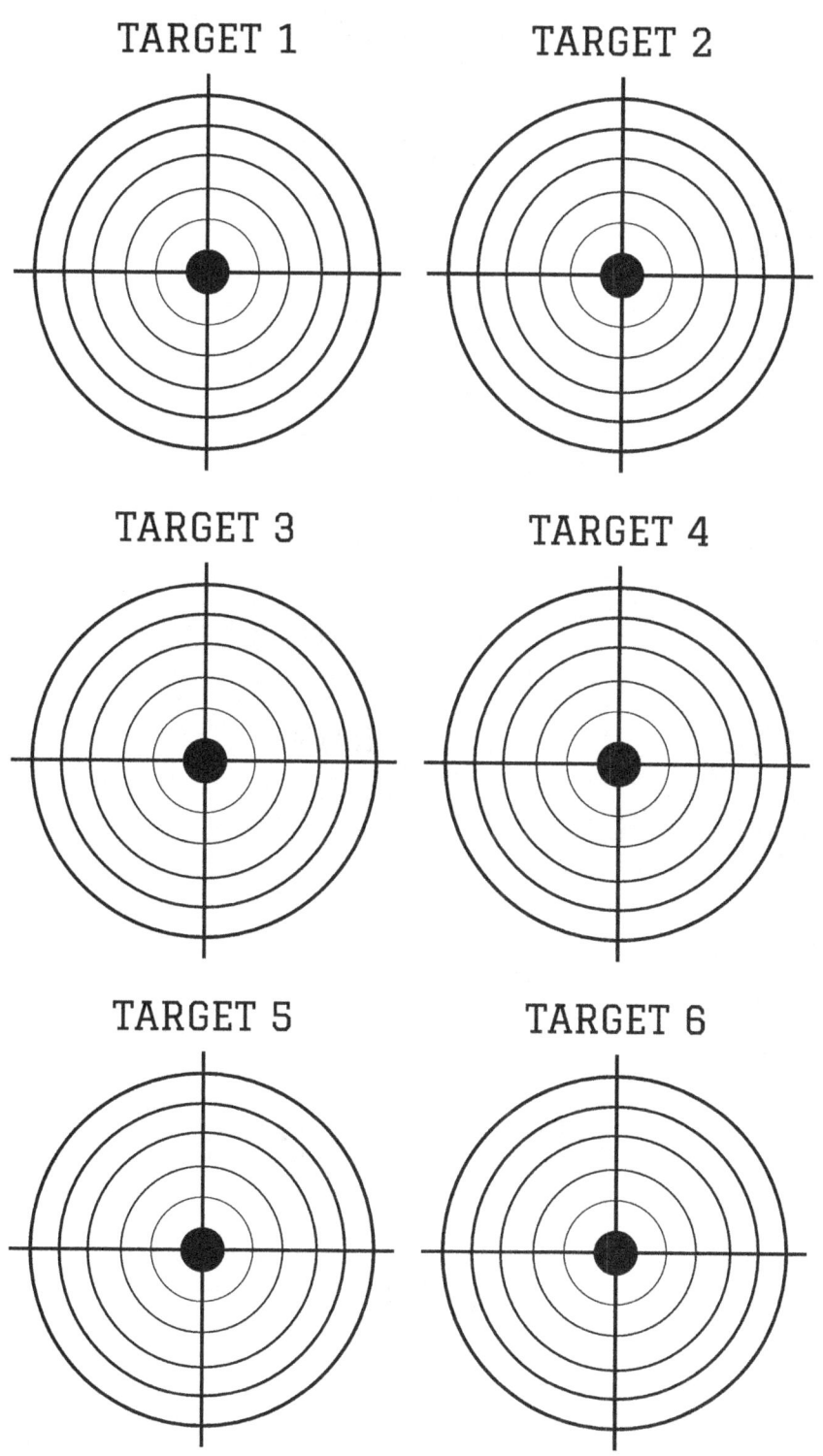

DATE / LOCATION: _____

CONDITIONS

WEATHER:

WIND:

SHOOTING

FIREARM:

BULLET: SEATING DEPTH:

POWDER: GRAINS:

PRIMER:

BRASS:

DISTANCE:

OVERALL RESULTS

★ ★ ★ ★ ★

NOTES

_____

_____

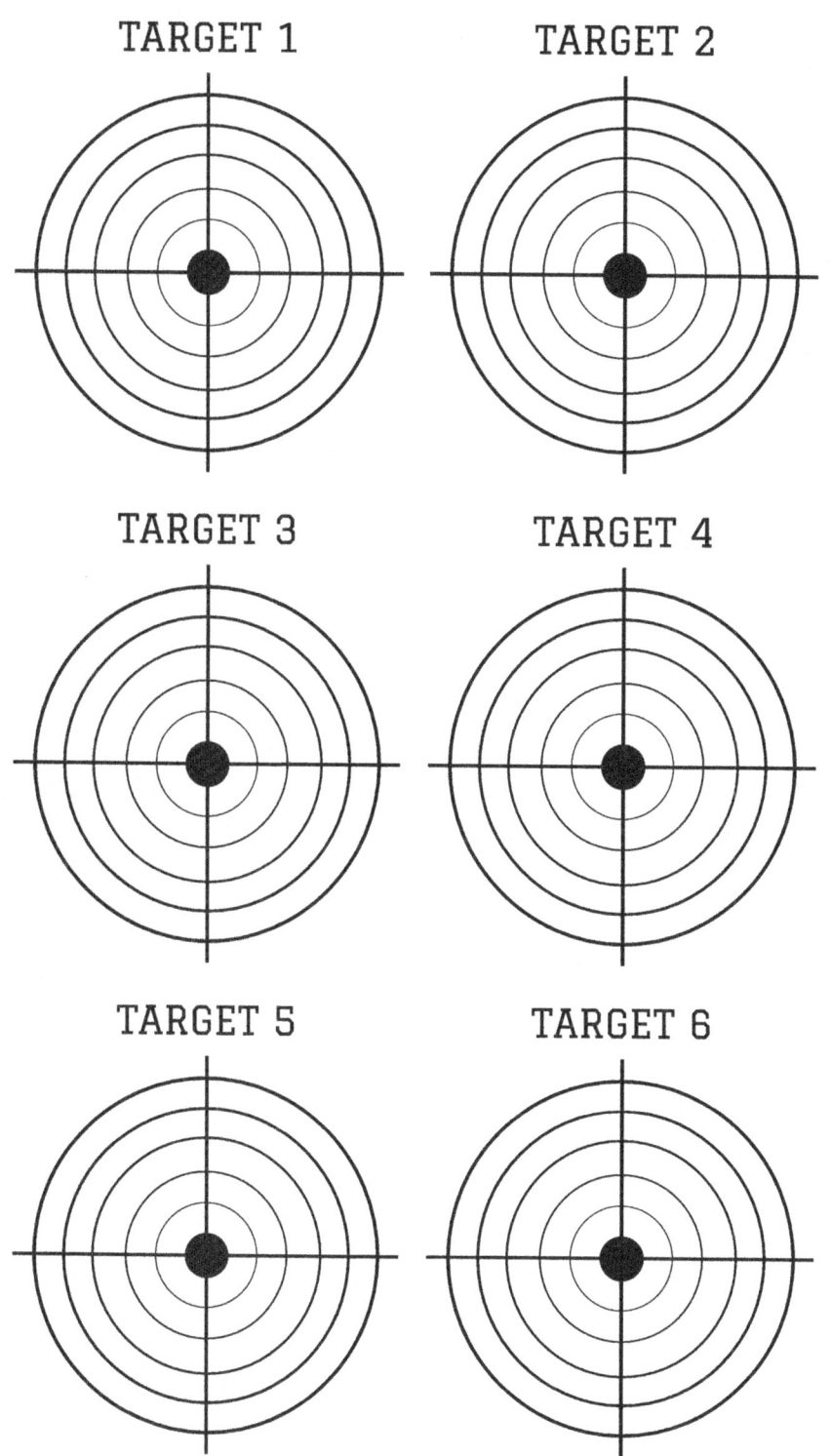

DATE / LOCATION: _____

CONDITIONS

WEATHER:

WIND:

SHOOTING

FIREARM:

BULLET:

SEATING DEPTH:

POWDER:

GRAINS:

PRIMER:

BRASS:

DISTANCE:

OVERALL RESULTS

★ ★ ★ ★ ★

NOTES

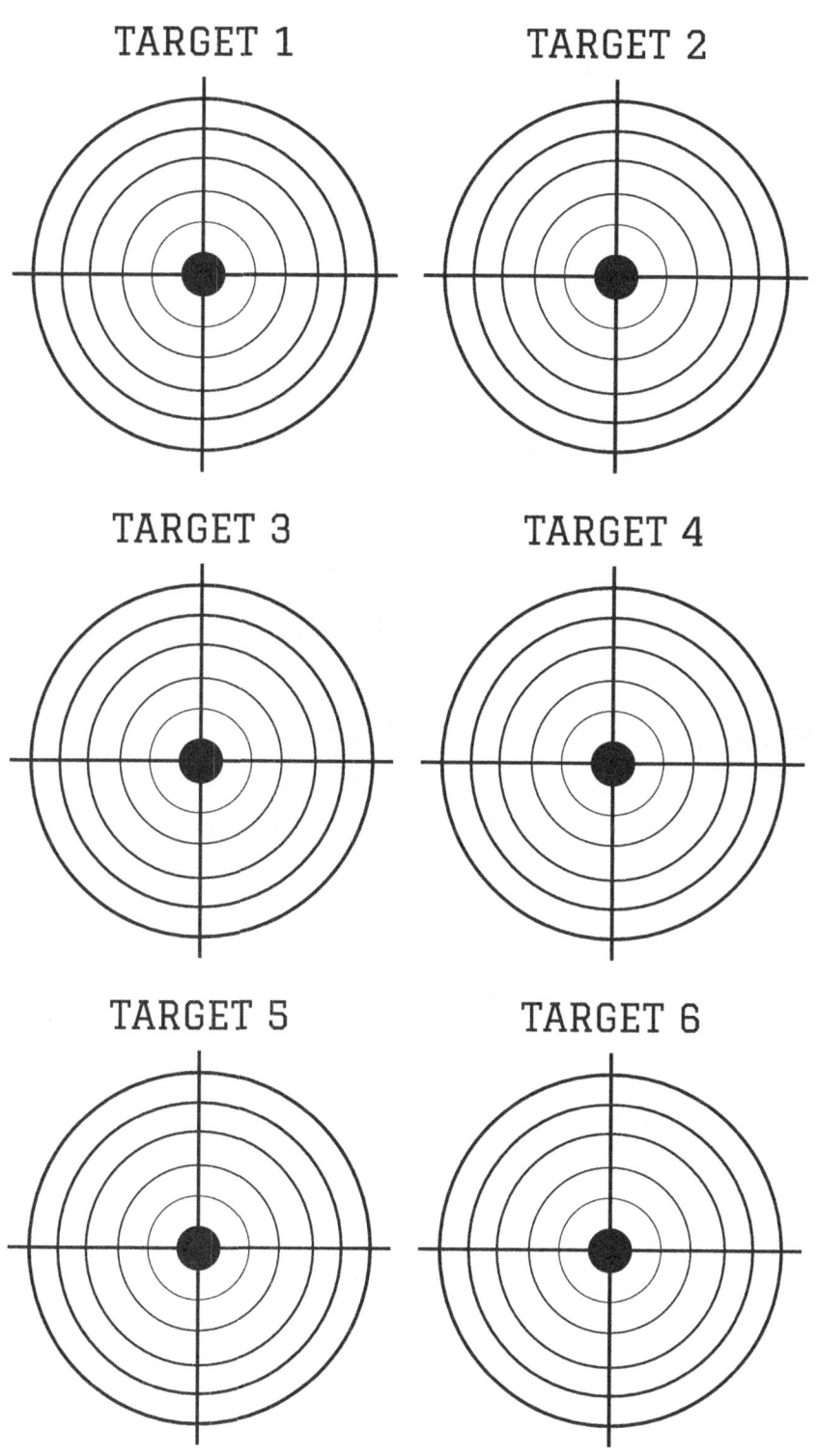

DATE / LOCATION: _____

CONDITIONS

WEATHER:

WIND:

SHOOTING

FIREARM:

BULLET:

SEATING DEPTH:

POWDER:

GRAINS:

PRIMER:

BRASS:

DISTANCE:

OVERALL RESULTS

★ ★ ★ ★ ★

NOTES

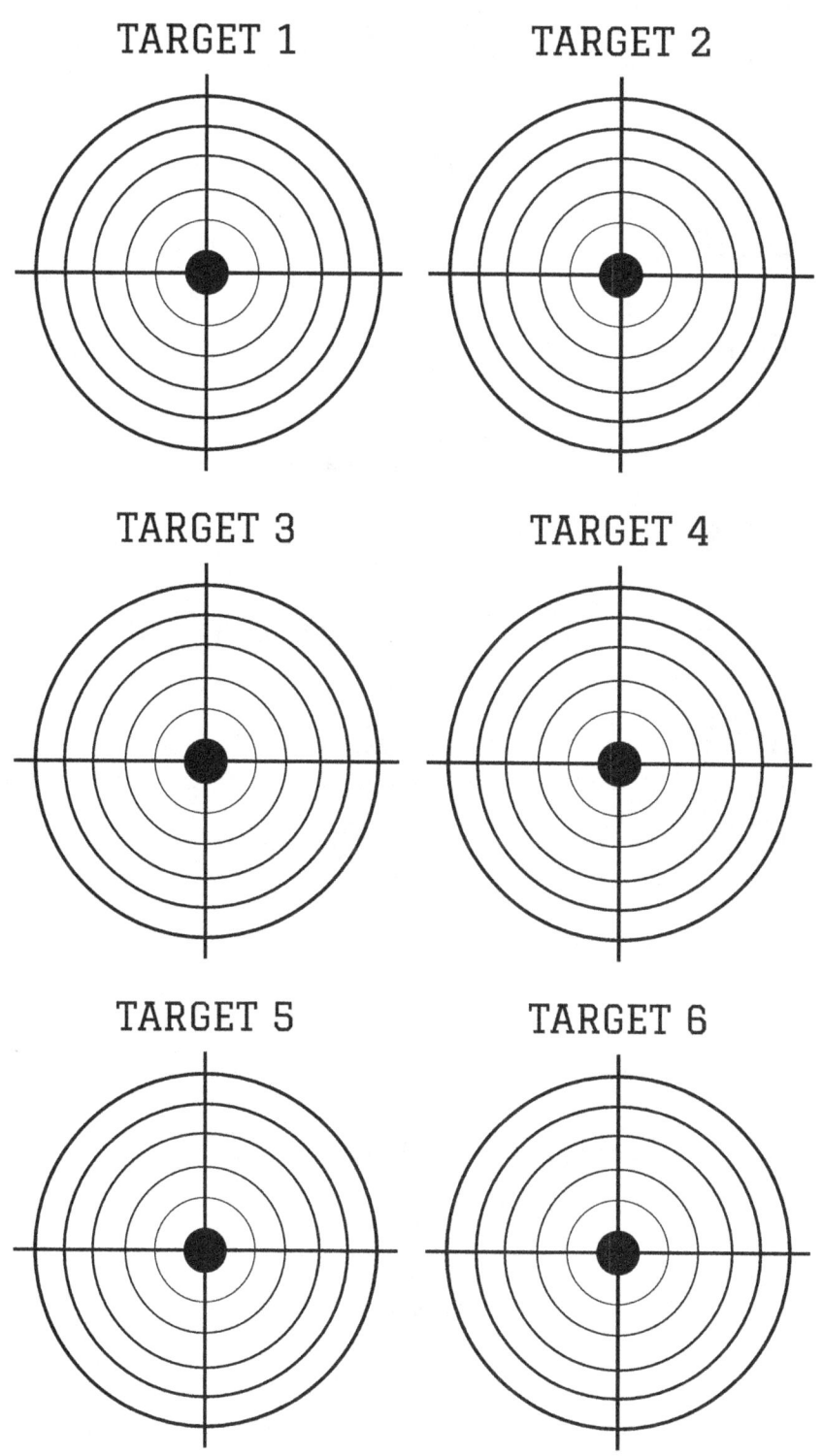

DATE / LOCATION: _____

CONDITIONS

WEATHER:

WIND:

SHOOTING

FIREARM:

BULLET: SEATING DEPTH:

POWDER: GRAINS:

PRIMER:

BRASS:

DISTANCE:

OVERALL RESULTS

☆ ☆ ☆ ☆ ☆

NOTES

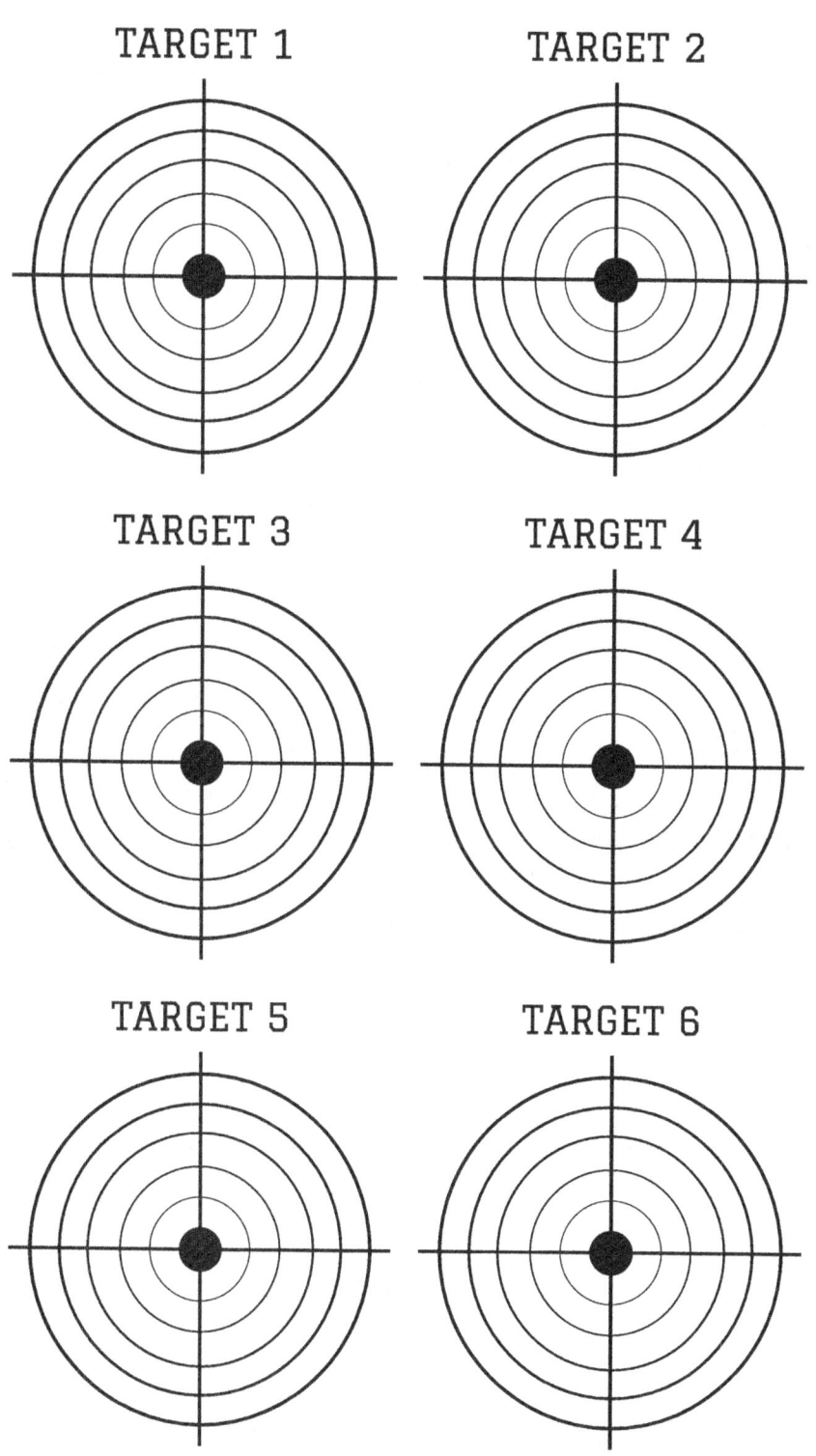

DATE / LOCATION: _____

CONDITIONS

WEATHER:

WIND:

SHOOTING

FIREARM:

BULLET:

SEATING DEPTH:

POWDER:

GRAINS:

PRIMER:

BRASS:

DISTANCE:

OVERALL RESULTS

★ ★ ★ ★ ★

NOTES

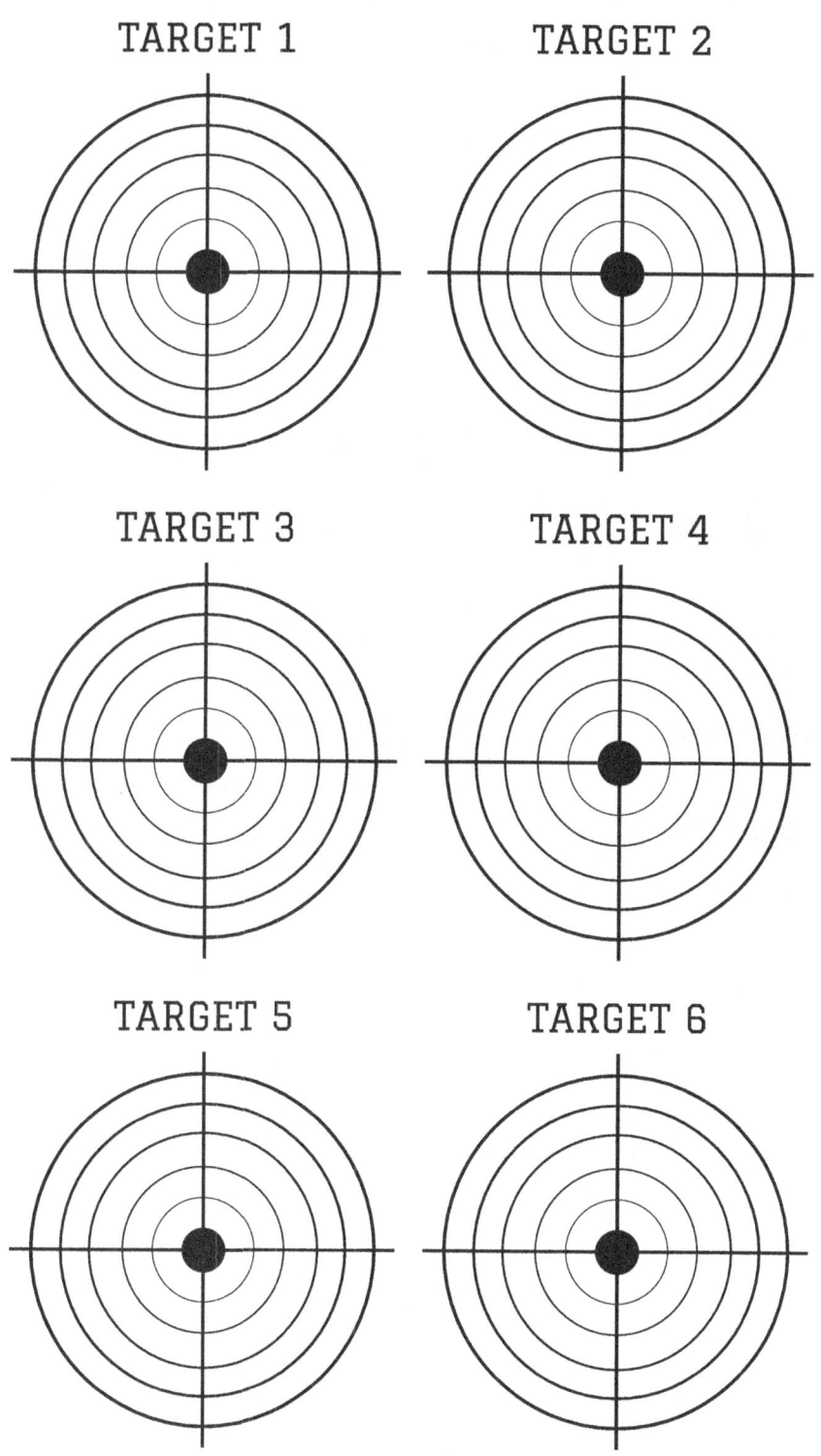

DATE / LOCATION: _____

CONDITIONS

WEATHER:

WIND:

SHOOTING

FIREARM:

BULLET:

SEATING DEPTH:

POWDER:

GRAINS:

PRIMER:

BRASS:

DISTANCE:

OVERALL RESULTS

★ ★ ★ ★ ★

NOTES

_____

_____

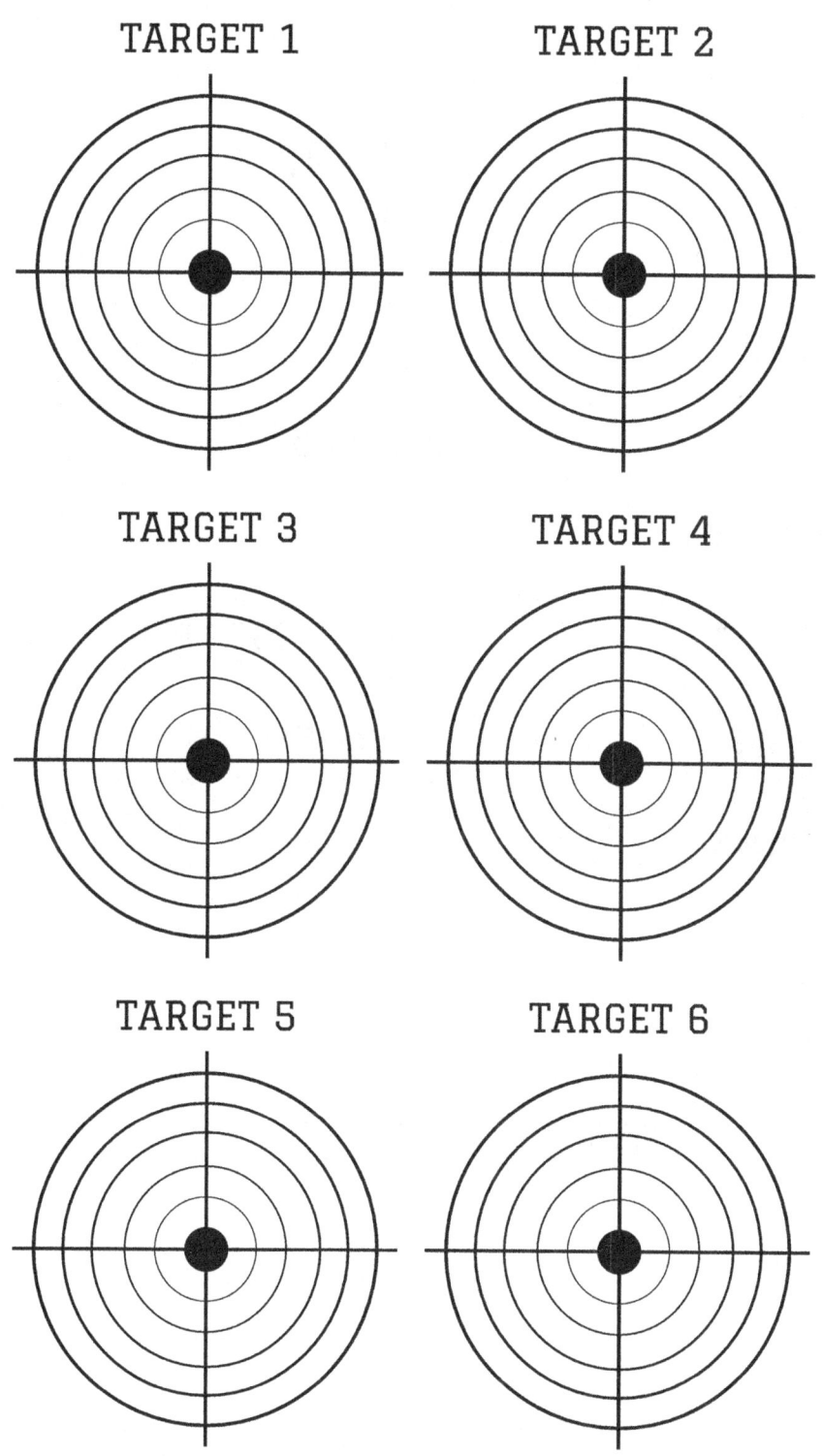

DATE / LOCATION: _____

CONDITIONS

WEATHER:

WIND:

SHOOTING

FIREARM:

BULLET: SEATING DEPTH:

POWDER: GRAINS:

PRIMER:

BRASS:

DISTANCE:

OVERALL RESULTS

★ ★ ★ ★ ★

NOTES

_____

_____

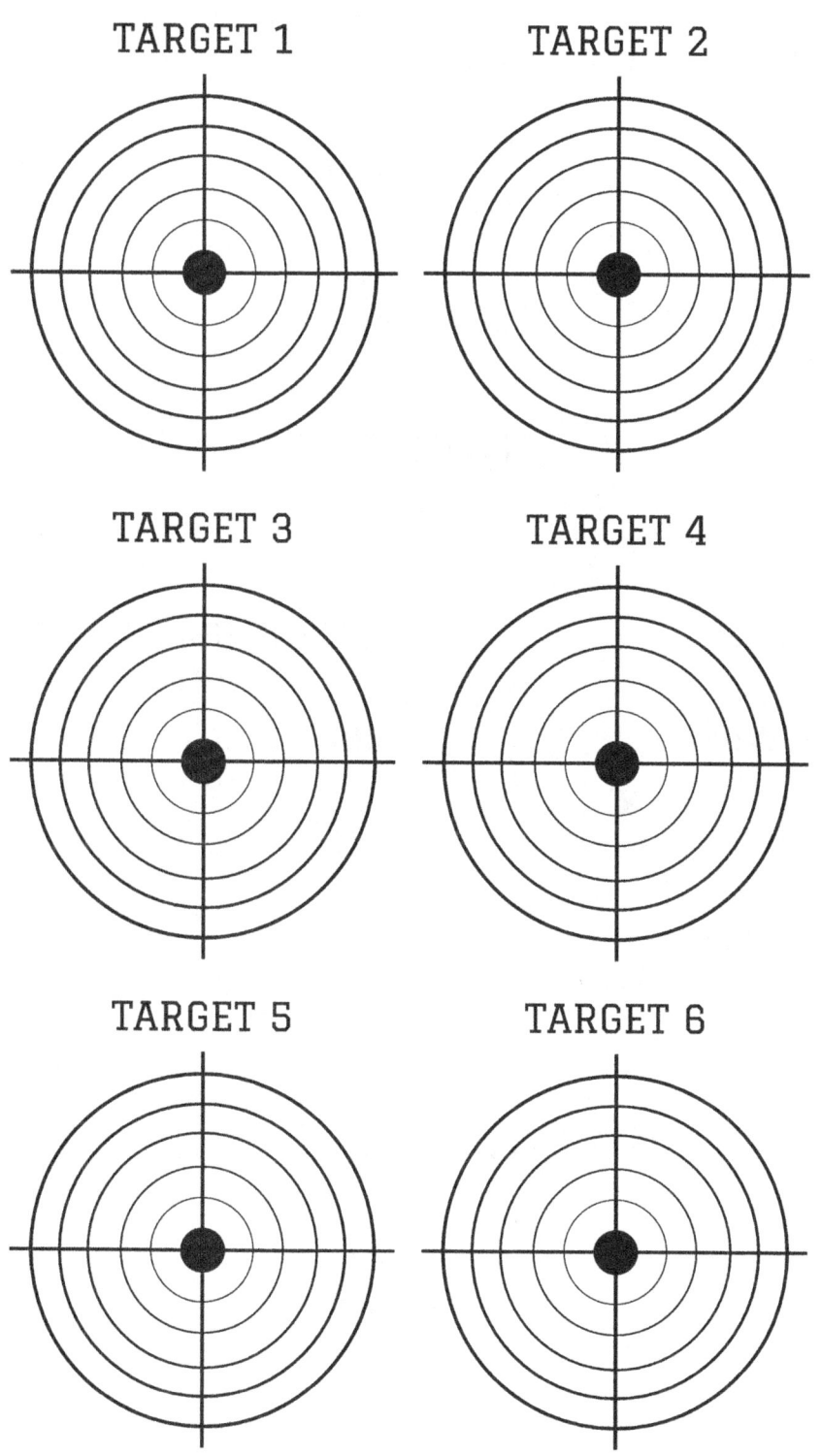

DATE / LOCATION: _____

CONDITIONS

WEATHER:

WIND:

SHOOTING

FIREARM:

BULLET: SEATING DEPTH:

POWDER: GRAINS:

PRIMER:

BRASS:

DISTANCE:

OVERALL RESULTS

★ ★ ★ ★ ★

NOTES

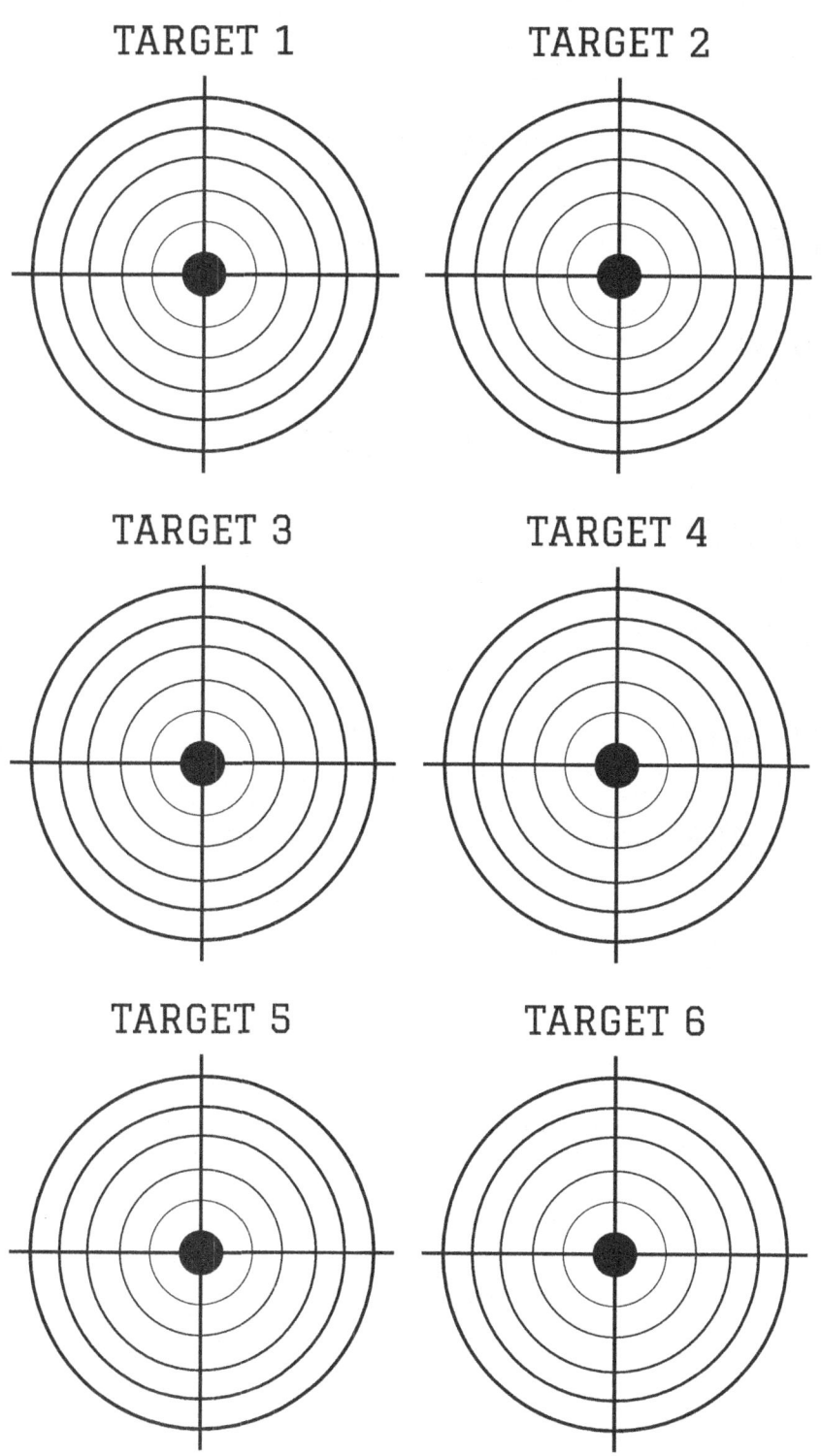

DATE / LOCATION: _____

CONDITIONS

WEATHER:

WIND:

SHOOTING

FIREARM:

BULLET: SEATING DEPTH:

POWDER: GRAINS:

PRIMER:

BRASS:

DISTANCE:

OVERALL RESULTS

☆ ☆ ☆ ☆ ☆

NOTES

_____

_____

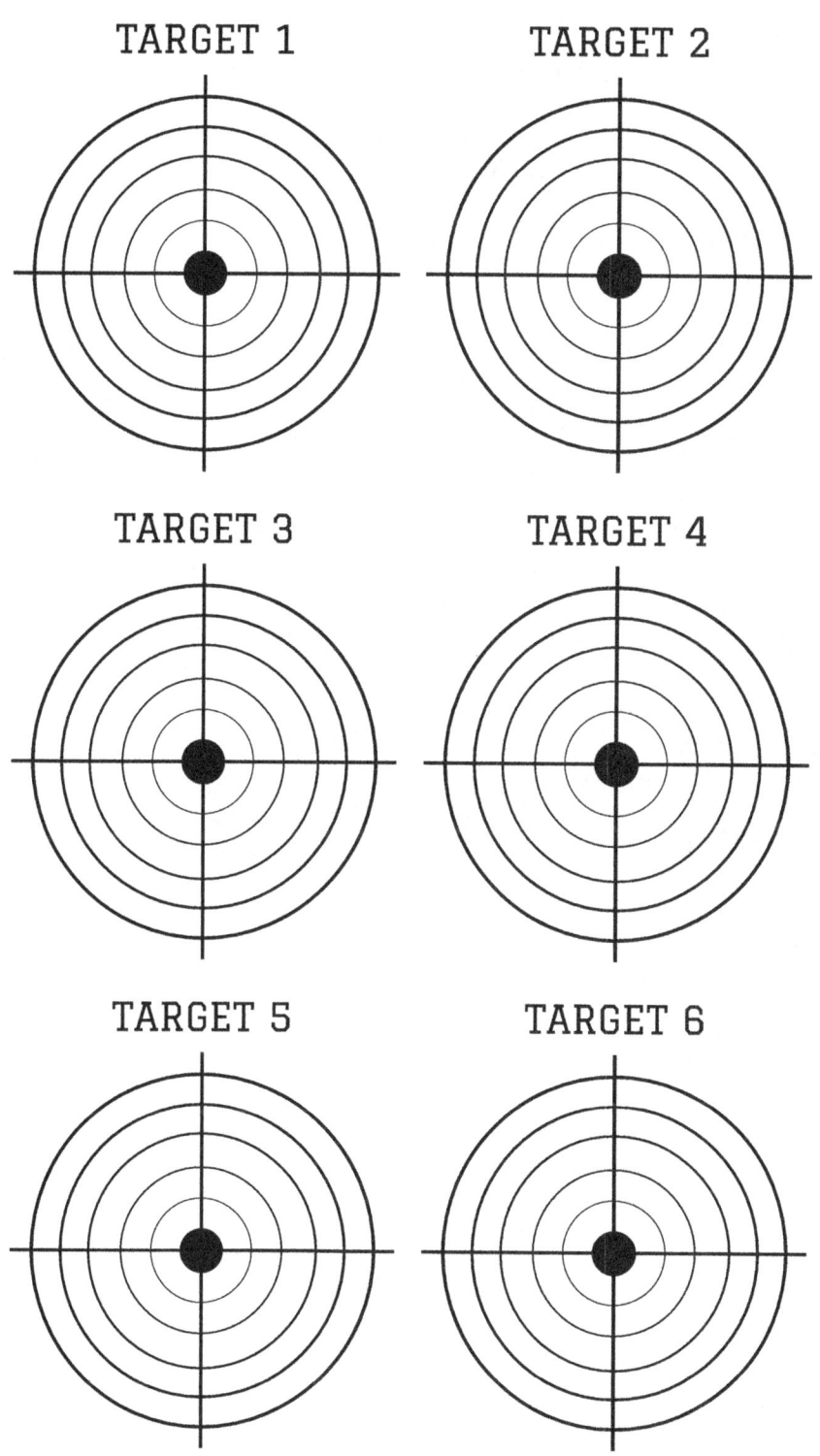

DATE / LOCATION: _____

CONDITIONS

WEATHER:

WIND:

SHOOTING

FIREARM:

BULLET: SEATING DEPTH:

POWDER: GRAINS:

PRIMER:

BRASS:

DISTANCE:

OVERALL RESULTS

☆ ☆ ☆ ☆ ☆

NOTES

_____

_____

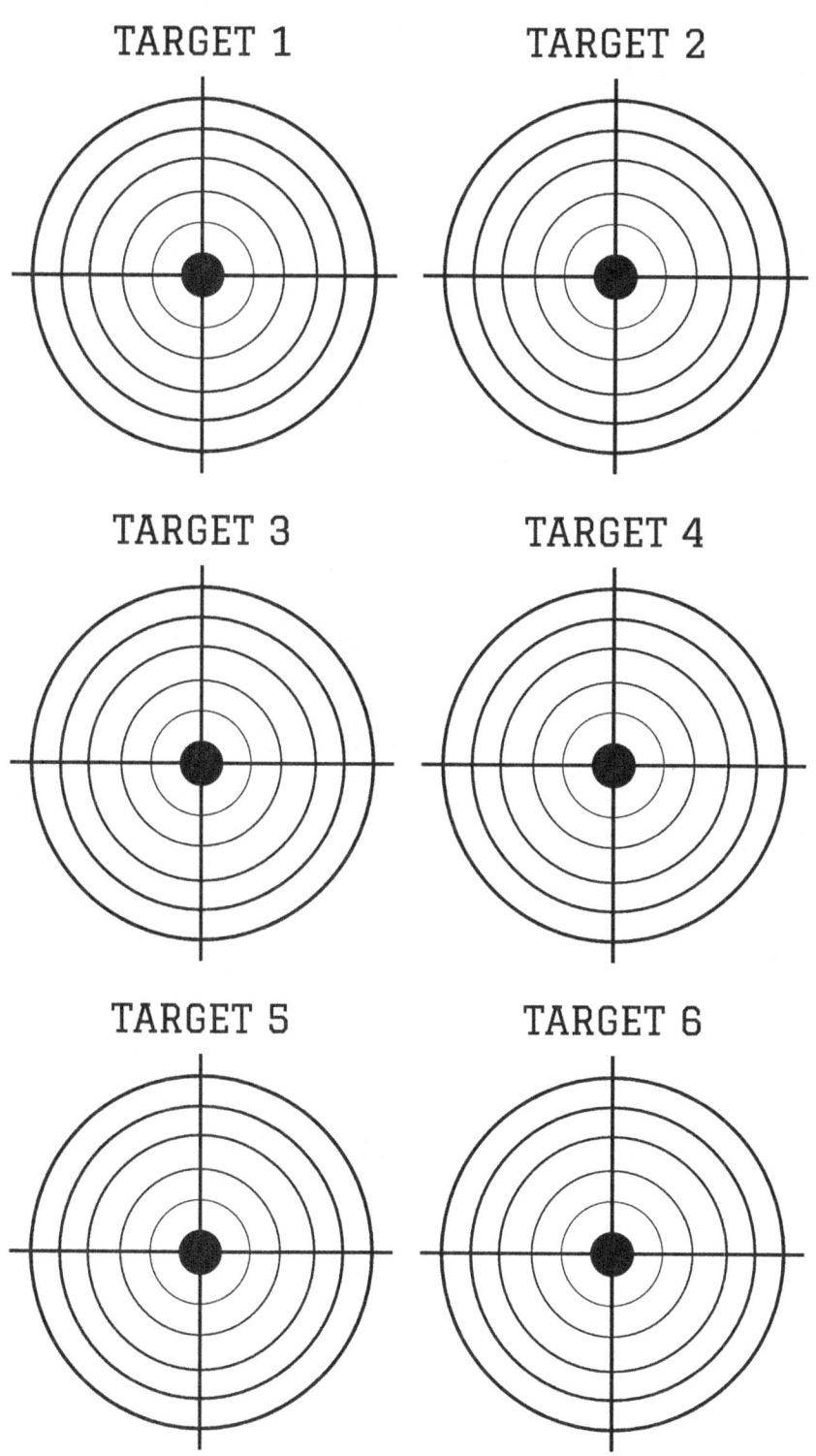

DATE / LOCATION: _____

CONDITIONS

WEATHER:

WIND:

SHOOTING

FIREARM:

BULLET:

SEATING DEPTH:

POWDER:

GRAINS:

PRIMER:

BRASS:

DISTANCE:

OVERALL RESULTS

★ ★ ★ ★ ★

NOTES

_____

_____

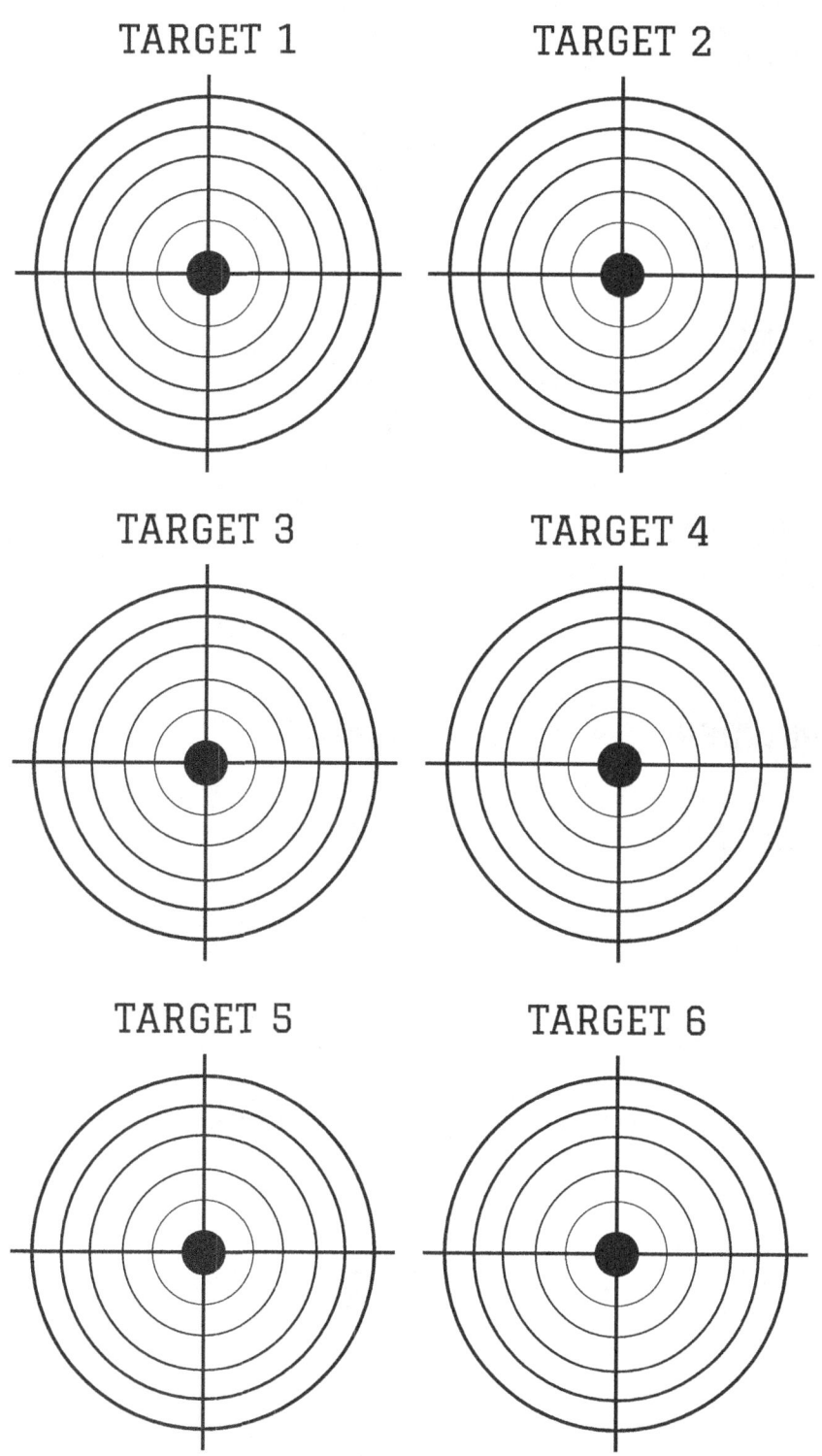

DATE / LOCATION: _____

CONDITIONS

WEATHER:

WIND:

SHOOTING

FIREARM:

BULLET:

SEATING DEPTH:

POWDER:

GRAINS:

PRIMER:

BRASS:

DISTANCE:

OVERALL RESULTS

★ ★ ★ ★ ★

NOTES

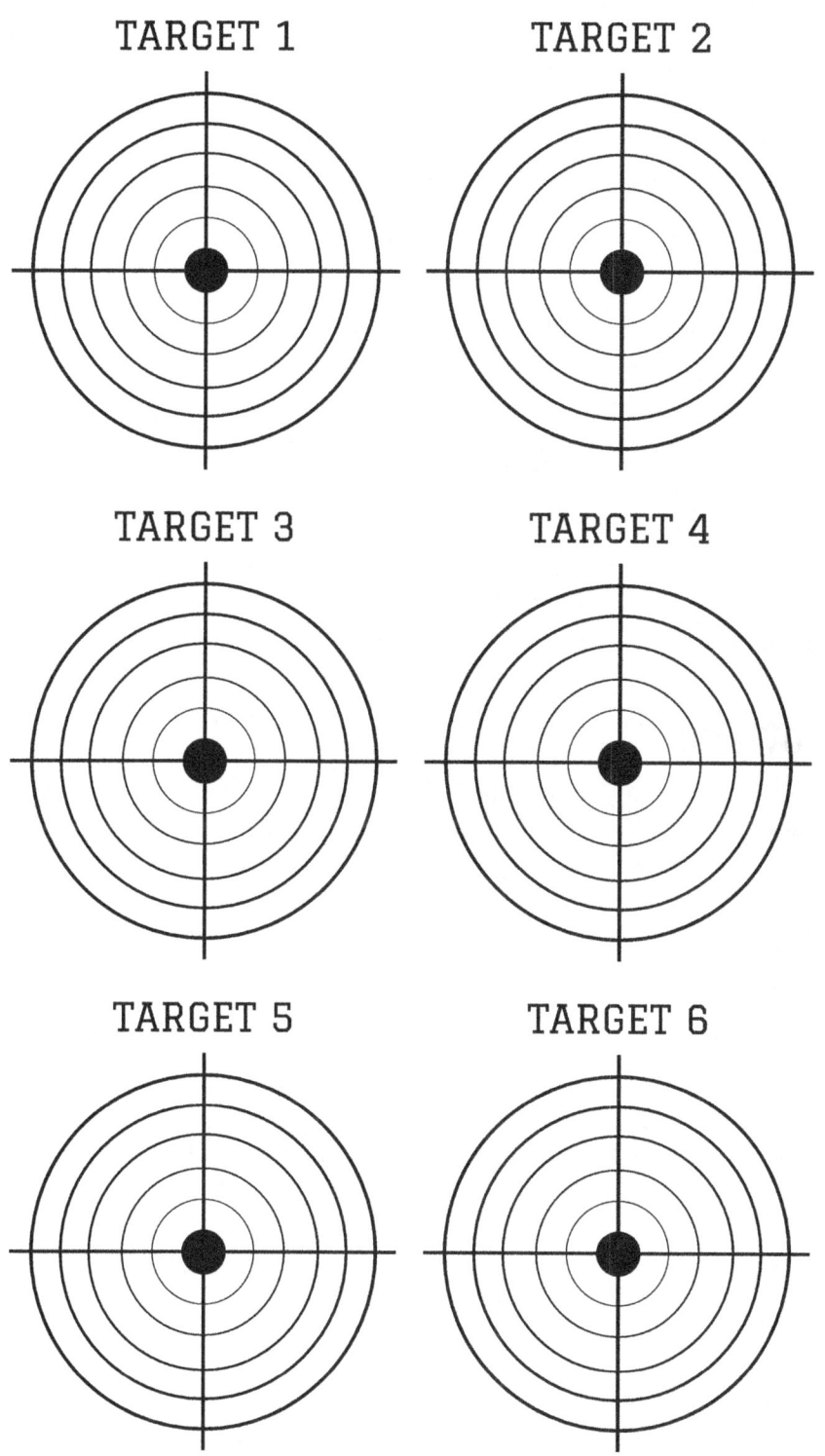

DATE / LOCATION: _____

CONDITIONS

WEATHER:

WIND:

SHOOTING

FIREARM:

BULLET: | SEATING DEPTH:

POWDER: | GRAINS:

PRIMER:

BRASS:

DISTANCE:

OVERALL RESULTS
★ ★ ★ ★ ★

NOTES

_____

_____

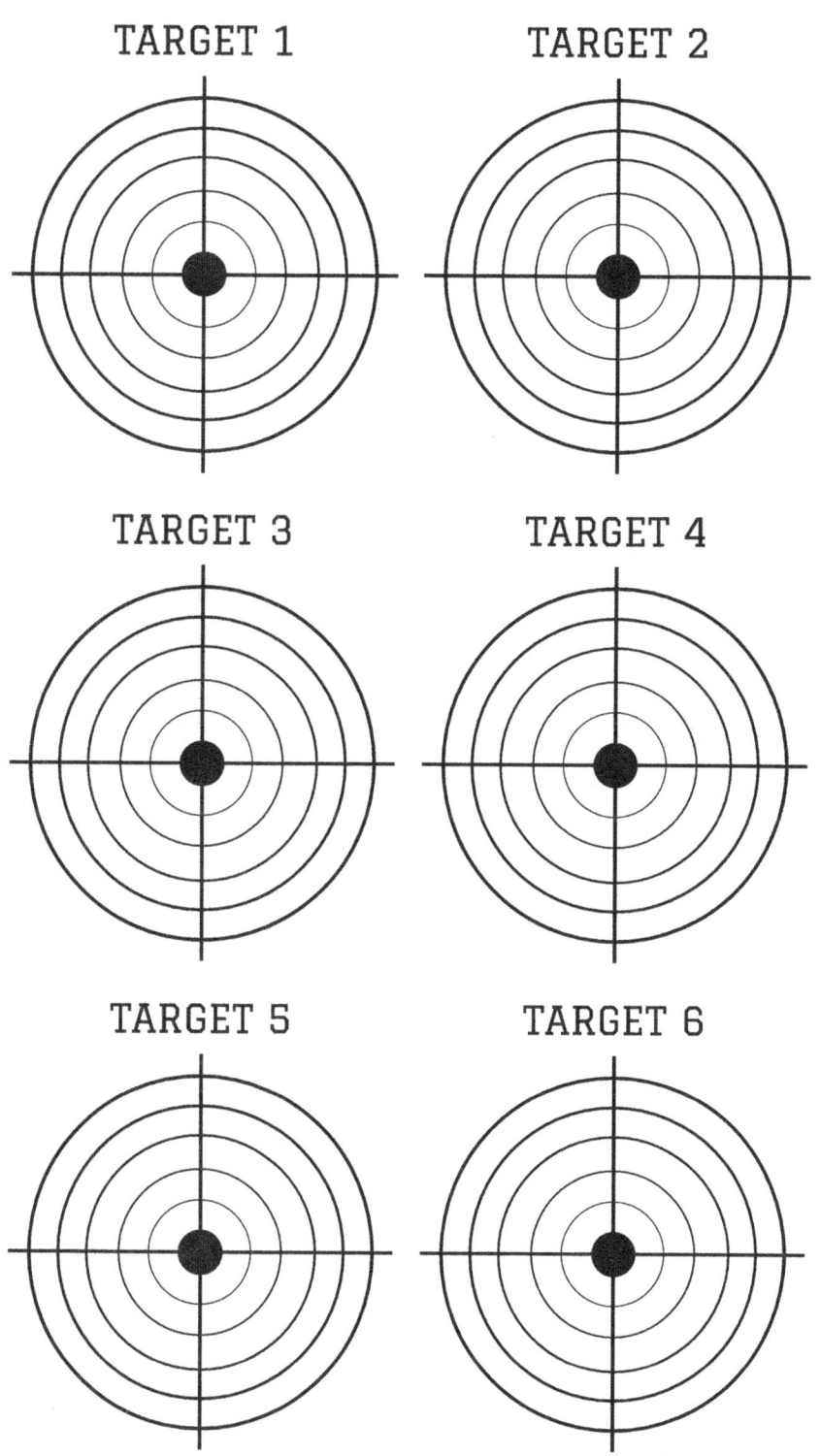

DATE / LOCATION: _____

CONDITIONS

WEATHER:

WIND:

SHOOTING

FIREARM:

BULLET: SEATING DEPTH:

POWDER: GRAINS:

PRIMER:

BRASS:

DISTANCE:

OVERALL RESULTS
★ ★ ★ ★ ★

NOTES

_____

_____

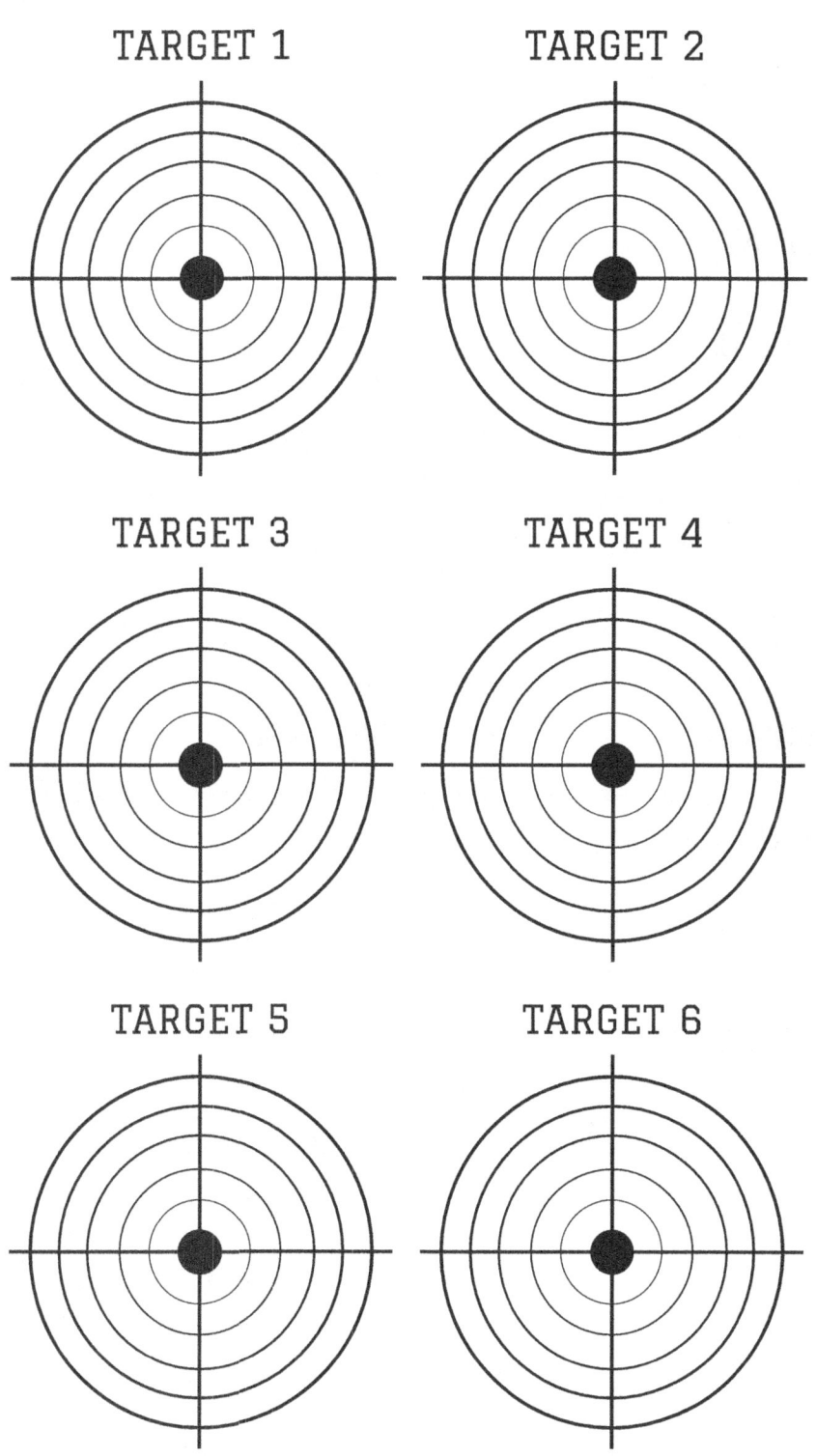

DATE / LOCATION: _____

CONDITIONS

WEATHER:

WIND:

SHOOTING

FIREARM:

BULLET:

SEATING DEPTH:

POWDER:

GRAINS:

PRIMER:

BRASS:

DISTANCE:

OVERALL RESULTS

★ ★ ★ ★ ★

NOTES

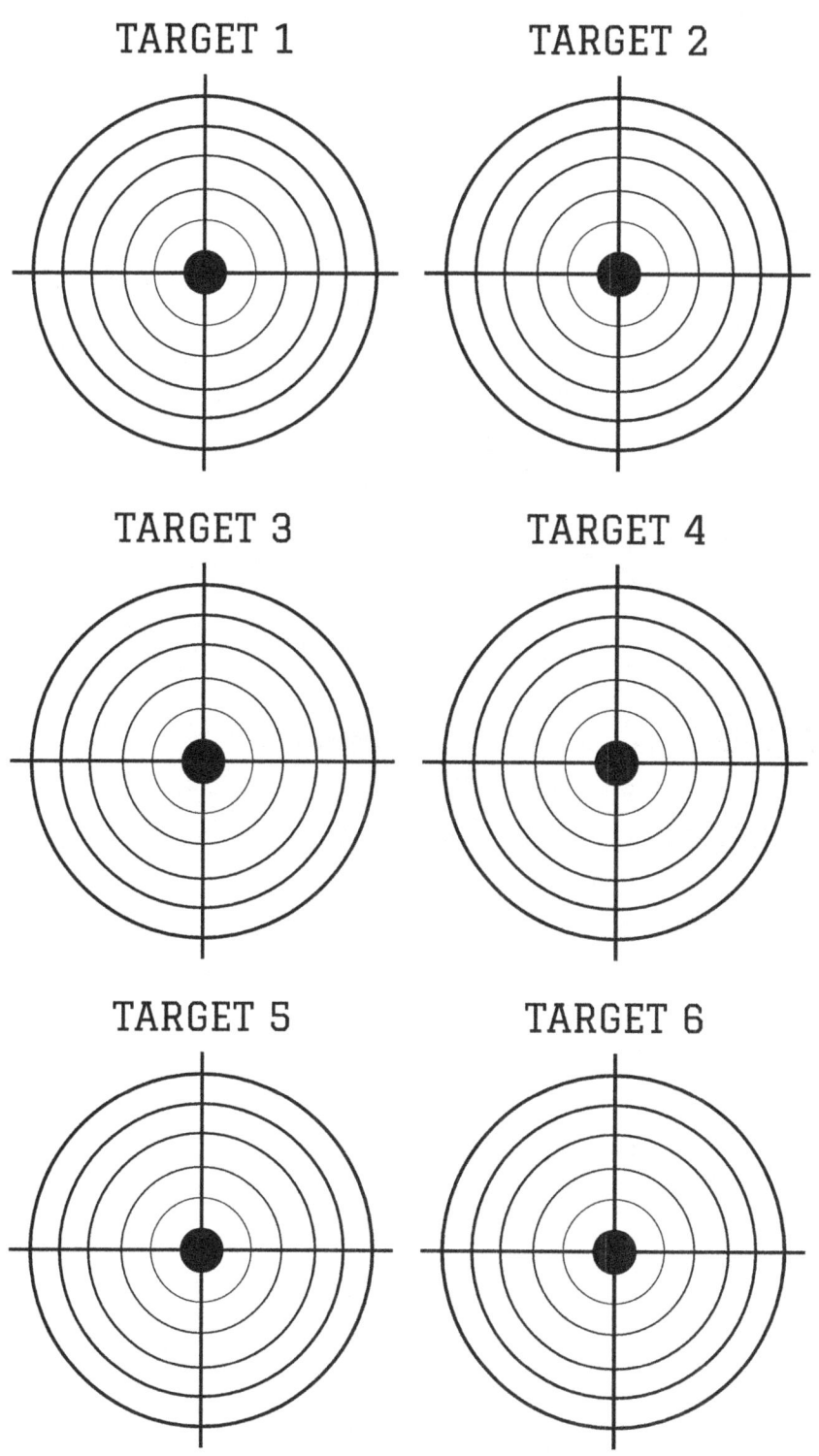

DATE / LOCATION: _____

CONDITIONS

WEATHER:

WIND:

SHOOTING

FIREARM:

BULLET: SEATING DEPTH:

POWDER: GRAINS:

PRIMER:

BRASS:

DISTANCE:

OVERALL RESULTS

★ ★ ★ ★ ★

NOTES

_____

_____

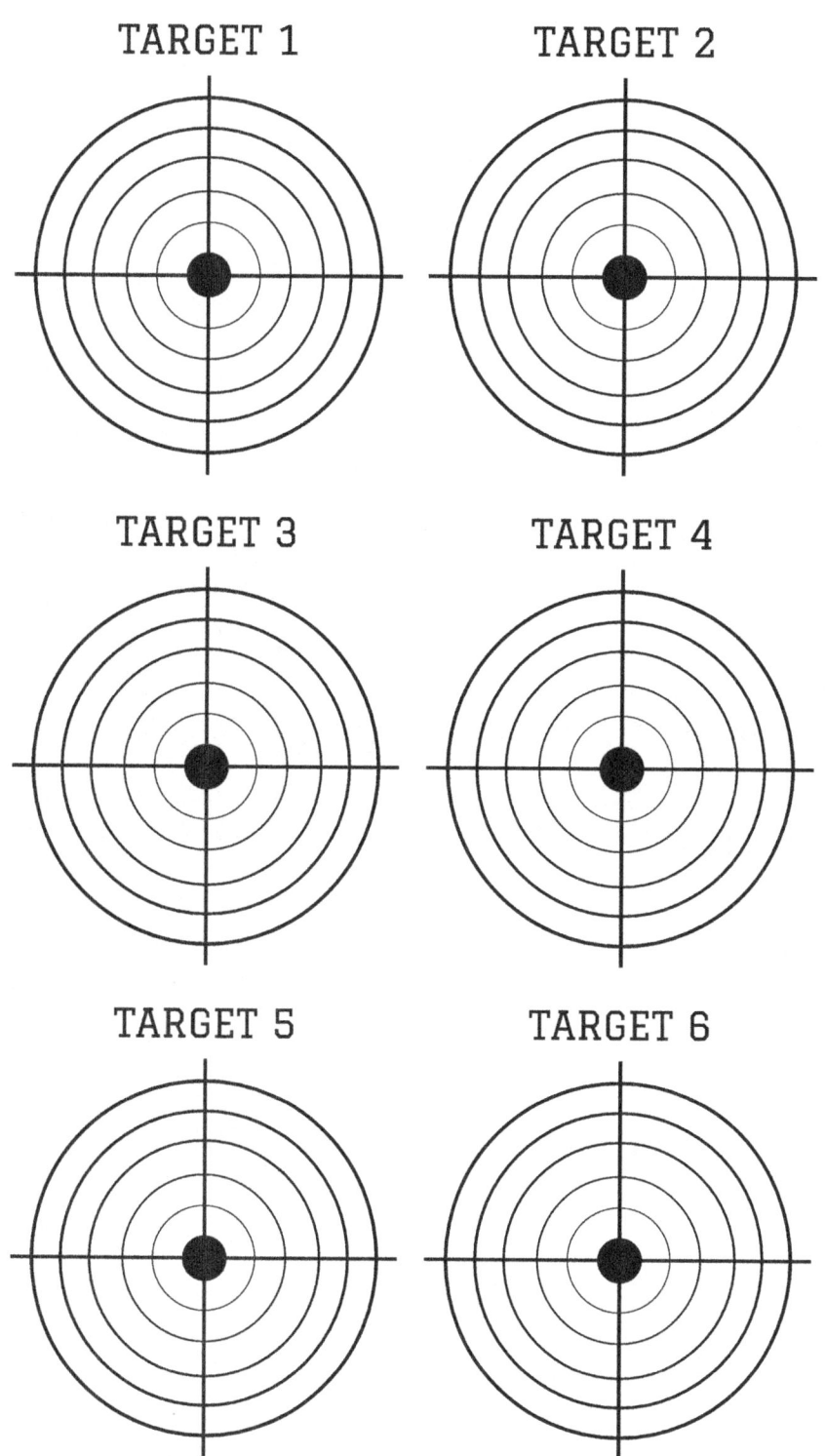

DATE / LOCATION: _____

CONDITIONS

WEATHER:

WIND:

SHOOTING

FIREARM:

BULLET: SEATING DEPTH:

POWDER: GRAINS:

PRIMER:

BRASS:

DISTANCE:

OVERALL RESULTS

★ ★ ★ ★ ★

NOTES

_____

_____

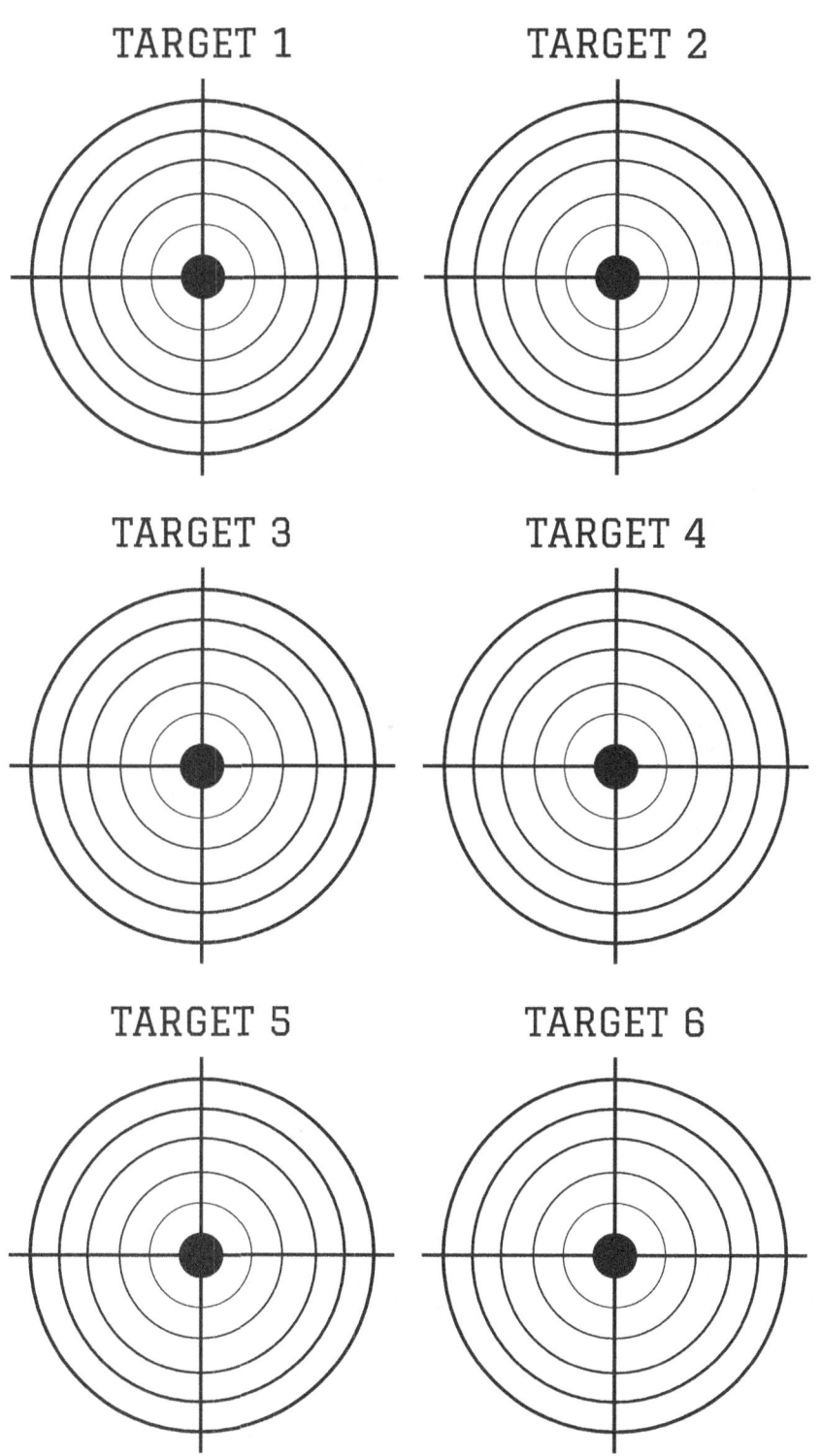

DATE / LOCATION: _____

CONDITIONS

WEATHER:

WIND:

SHOOTING

FIREARM:

BULLET:

SEATING DEPTH:

POWDER:

GRAINS:

PRIMER:

BRASS:

DISTANCE:

OVERALL RESULTS

★ ★ ★ ★ ★

NOTES

_____

_____

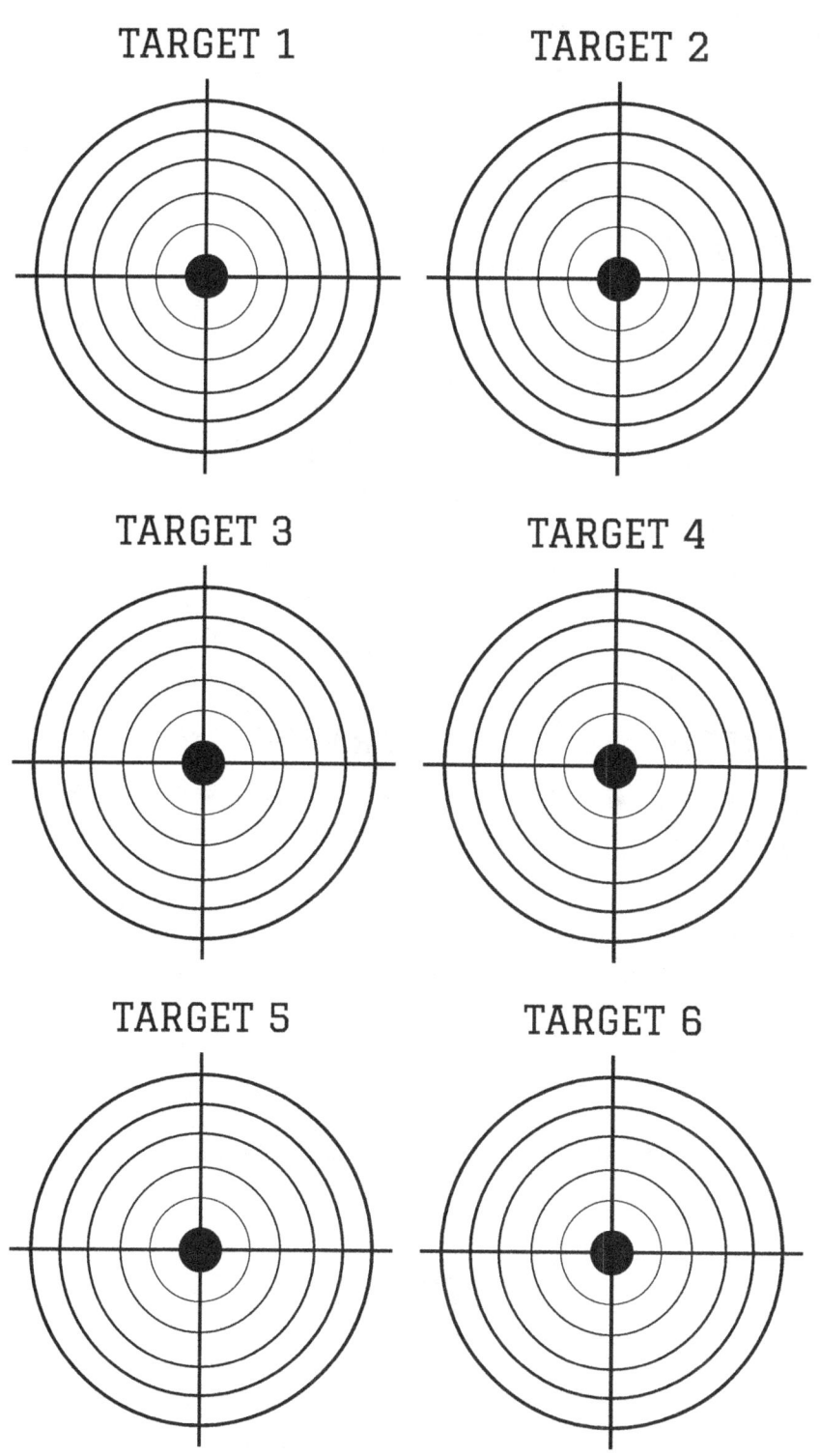

DATE / LOCATION: _____

CONDITIONS

WEATHER:

WIND:

SHOOTING

FIREARM:

BULLET: SEATING DEPTH:

POWDER: GRAINS:

PRIMER:

BRASS:

DISTANCE:

OVERALL RESULTS
★ ★ ★ ★ ★

NOTES

_____

_____

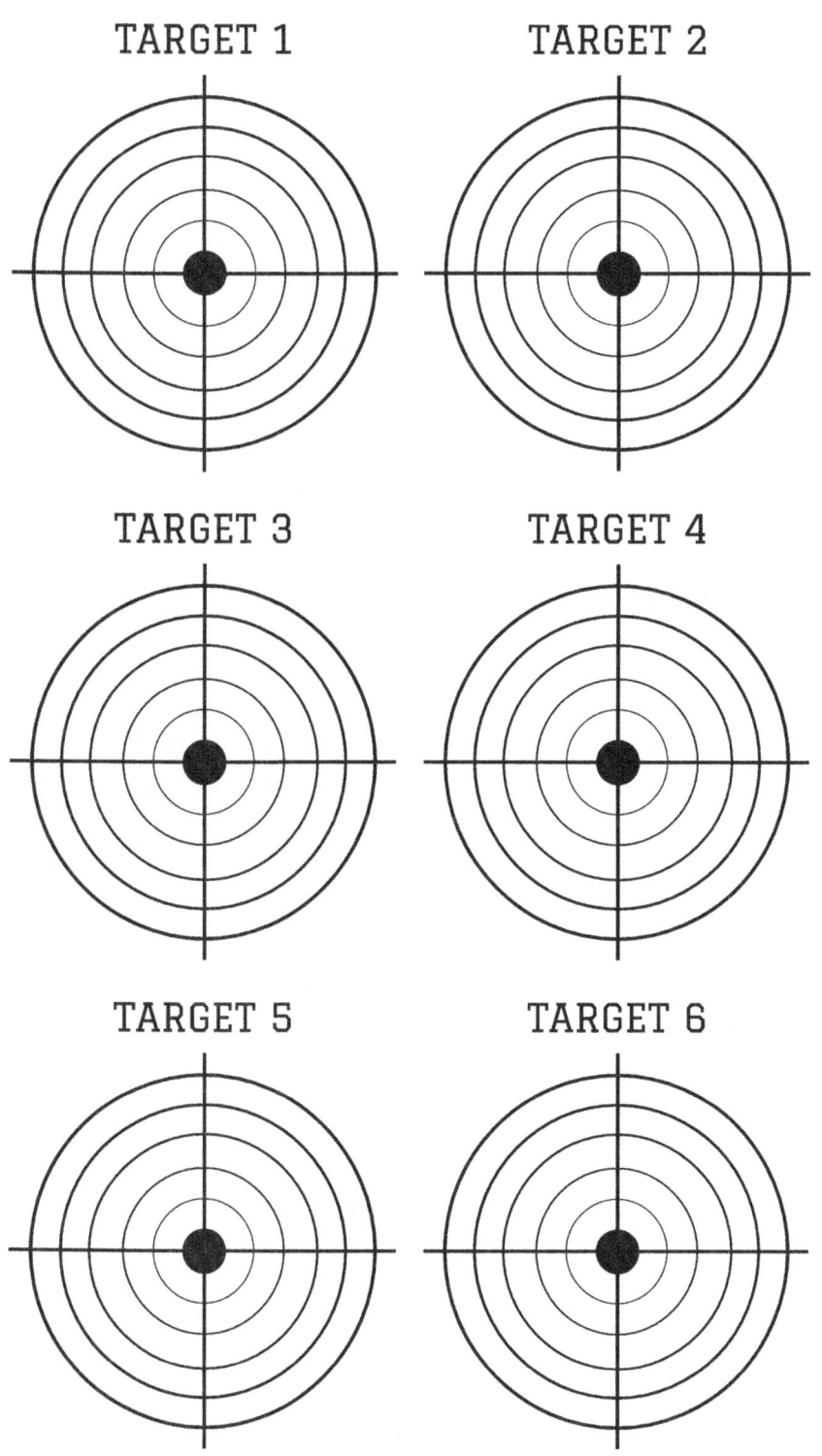

Made in the USA
Las Vegas, NV
07 February 2024

85438038R00059